What *Dads* Need to Know about *Daughters*

What *Moms* Need to Know about *Sons*

T0106218

**What *Dads*
Need to Know
about *Daughters***

**What *Moms*
Need to Know
about *Sons***

BESTSELLING AUTHORS
**John and
Helen Burns**

HOWARD BOOKS
A DIVISION OF SIMON & SCHUSTER
New York   London   Toronto   Sydney

Our purpose at Howard Books is to:
• *Increase faith* in the hearts of growing Christians
• *Inspire holiness* in the lives of believers
• *Instill hope* in the hearts of struggling people everywhere
Because He's coming again!

Published by Howard Books, a division of Simon & Schuster, Inc.
1230 Avenue of the Americas, New York, NY 10020
www.howardpublishing.com

What Dads Need to Know about Daughters/What Moms Need to Know about Sons © 2007 by John and Helen Burns

Library of Congress Cataloging-in-Publication Data is available.

ISBN 13: 978-1-4516-4334-3

10 9 8 7 6 5 4 3

HOWARD colophon is a registered trademark of Simon & Schuster, Inc.

Manufactured in the United States of America

For information regarding special discounts for bulk purchases, please contact: Simon & Schuster Special Sales at 1-800-456-6798 or business@simonandschuster.com.

Edited by Michelle Buckingham
Cover design by The Design Works
Interior design by Stephanie D. Walker
Photography by photos.com (pp. i, iii. xii, xiii, 1, 7, 25, 41, 63, 77, 78–79, 83, 95) and Chrys Howard (pp. i, iii, 2–3, 77, 115, 133)

Contents

Contents

Part 2: What Dads Need to Know about Daughters by Helen Burns

Preface

Someone once said it takes a community to raise a child. My wife, Helen, and I tend to agree. We need male and female; we need moms and dads; we need older and younger. We need the wisdom of those who have already gone before us, who've already experienced what we're going through. And I believe we need books like this.

If you are a mother reading this book, we want to congratulate you, and we want to celebrate you. You are our hero. You are every son's hero. You are the answer to so much of the pain in our world today.

If you are a dad reading this book, we salute you. You're a hero and every daughter's dream. You are the answer to the cries of a broken world.

God created us male and female on purpose. His plan was that men and women would work together to complete one another, and the result would be "very good." Into this plan God designed a few significant challenges, however. Why? So that we would enjoy the great victory and reward that comes from overcoming these challenges as we build healthy relationships, families, and generations. Great victories only come through great challenges! The good news is that the God who designed these challenges also designed us with the capacity to overcome them.

That means every challenge has a God-given answer. Boys face many obstacles along their journey toward manhood, and the answers are often found in Mom. Girls encounter questions along their journey toward womanhood, and the keys are often found in Dad.

What does that mean for moms and dads? Big adventures of course! That's why we've written this book in two parts. For mothers, I have written *What Moms Need to Know about Sons*. For fathers, Helen has written *What Dads Need to Know about Daughters*. Many parenting principles apply to both moms and dads, sons and daughters, and many great parenting books are available to teach these principles. Our purpose in writing this two-for-one book is not to duplicate what others have written. Rather, it's to focus specifically on a mother's role in the lives of her sons and a father's role in the lives of his daughters. Yes, sons need great dads; but sons also profit from wise, loving mothers who understand the unique requirements boys have for maternal care, encouragement, and support. Great moms are a *must* for daughters, but they also need wise, loving fathers who understand the unique needs girls have for fatherly love, protection, and affirmation.

Proverbs 24:3–4 tells us, "Through skillful and godly Wisdom is a house (a life, a home, a family) built, and by understanding it is established [on a sound and good foundation], and by knowledge shall its chambers [of every area] be filled with all precious and pleasant riches" (AMP). In order to build our families with wisdom, we must first gather the pertinent knowledge. Helen and I pray that this book will help provide some of that knowledge. We pray it will help promote greater understanding between moms and sons, between dads and daughters, and between males and females in general.

And we pray for *you*—that you will have all the knowledge and understanding you need to build a "sound and good foundation" for your life, your home, your family, and the generations to come. Nothing less than the future of the world depends upon it.

Snips and snails, and puppy dog tails.
That's what little boys are made of!
Sugar and spice and all things nice.
That's what little girls are made of.

—A Mother Goose Nursery Rhyme

The Difference between Boys and Girls

I (John) grew up in a family with five brothers and five sisters. From the perspective of a sibling, I understood early on that boys and girls are different. With my brothers I could wrestle and fight and play rough, but not with my sisters. If I played with my sisters that way, I was in big trouble with Mom and Dad. In those days I wasn't interested in trying to understand the differences between the sexes—just surviving them.

I always had more fun with my brothers than with my sisters. With my brothers I would go outside and hunt for snakes, frogs, caterpillars, and anything else that was unusual or weird. With my sisters I would end up playing house and being somebody's baby, brother, or daddy. How boring! I couldn't understand why girls thought it was fun to stay inside pretending to be an ordinary family doing ordinary things, when there were mud puddles, ant hills, and climbing trees outside waiting to be explored. I didn't spend too much time thinking about it though. I didn't need to understand the differences between boys and girls to be glad I was a boy!

Then I married Helen—and while I was still glad to be a boy, it didn't take long for my lack of understanding of the female sex to get me into trouble. Several years into my marriage, I was forced to realize I didn't understand my wife at all. In fact, quite unwittingly, I had done enough things wrong to nearly bankrupt our relationship. I was only doing what came naturally as a red-blooded male—having sex, going fishing, going golfing, going skiing, having sex, playing some more, and having sex some more. It didn't occur to me that Helen, as a red-blooded woman, might have needs and desires that were different than my own.

Suddenly it became imperative for me to understand the differences between male and female—not just the ones on the outside, but the ones on the inside too. That was the only way I was going to make my marriage work. After all, how can you successfully love someone if you don't understand how she thinks, feels, and communicates? How can you successfully meet her needs if you don't know what she wants? Thus began my journey of discovery to understand this whole other world called "female."

My original motivation was to understand my wife and rebuild my marriage. Then God blessed Helen and me with three wonderful daughters, and my inspiration went up another notch. In order to love, protect, and provide for my girls, I poured myself into this fascinating study of the differences between the sexes. Having completed coursework in biology, physiology, and psychology (I graduated as a dentist from the University of British Columbia in 1978), I was intrigued by the medical research. But my faith in God and total dependence on the Bible as the Word of God became the real anchor of my developing comprehension of God's ingenious, eternal plan.

Why Are We So Different?

I have to admit, in the early stages of my study, I was so amazed by the striking differences between male and female that I thought, *Maybe God is playing a joke on mankind.* He made men and women so different, so opposite, and yet so reliant upon each other! He created us with a very complex and complicated inter-dependence—and he did it *on purpose*.

Here are four key biblical and physiological facts I discovered.

God Created Man to Have Needs

Genesis 1 and 2 tell us the story of Creation. God created the stars, the earth, the animals, the whole universe—but his crowning achievement was man. Adam was complete and perfect in every way. He was superintelligent. Psychologists say that the average person today uses only a small fraction of his or her mental capacity. Adam used one hundred percent. Since Adam, generations of sickness, disease, and mutation have diminished mankind's brain-power; but Adam, the first man, operated at his full, God-created capacity. Not only was he able to name every species that God created, he was also able to remember them! (I struggle to remember the names of the people in our church.) In order to name the species, he first had to study them, since the purpose of each name was to describe its function. That means that Adam was the first and most brilliant zoologist of all time.

In addition to being smart, Adam was rich. Except for one tree in the middle of the garden in which he lived, everything belonged to him. He was the world's first and wealthiest landlord. If owning things could bring fulfillment, then Adam was the most fulfilled person in human history.

But there is something more fulfilling than possessions, and Adam had that too: a deep, intimate, ongoing relationship with God. He walked and talked with God every day in the garden. God was his Father, his mentor, and his friend. If all a man needs is God, then surely Adam was the most satisfied person that ever lived!

Amazingly, God thought otherwise.

From our point of view, Adam's life was perfect. He was brilliant, productive, wealthy, *and* he had a great relationship with God. If ever there was a person who could have said, "I don't need anyone else," it was Adam. But God said in Genesis 2:18, "It is not good that man should be alone; I will make him a helper comparable to him."

You see, Adam was created in the image of God, and "God is love" (1 John 4:16). Love is also an action verb that requires an object. Love gives, and Adam needed someone to give his life to. God paraded every species of animal before Adam to see if he could find one that would be suitable for him or comparable to him. But in all of God's creation, no creature was found that could cure Adam's aloneness.

So God put Adam to sleep and took something out of him.

I was a dentist before I became a pastor; and as a dentist, before I pulled a child's tooth, I always explained the anesthesia process by saying, "I'm going to put your tooth to sleep." The reason I anesthetized the tooth was because I was about to perform an operation that would be uncomfortable. When God was about to take something out of Adam, he put him to sleep. He knew he was about to create a need in Adam's life—a need that would be uncomfortable, even painful.

The result of that operation was that Adam could no longer say, "I don't need anyone." When he awoke, something was missing in Adam's life, and he needed someone to fill that aching void. Ever since, men have been searching for what is missing from their lives. We are often led to think—boys especially—that it is weak to need someone. It is not weak to have needs. It is human. God created us to need each other.

God Created Woman to Cure Man's Aloneness

With the rib he removed from Adam, God fashioned a woman. This woman was God's answer to Adam's aloneness. Eve was the "someone" Adam needed, the "someone" he was searching for to fill the void created intentionally by God. She was what was missing in his life! You see, aloneness is a heart ailment that can only be cured by relationship. So God put the answer to Adam's aloneness in Eve's heart by creating her with a special gift for building relationships. Since Eve, the desire and ability to create and complete families, communities, and generations has been a treasure God has hidden deep inside every woman—and his plan is that every man should go on a lifelong treasure hunt.

In God's economy, the way to receive is to give. For Adam to receive the treasure that was in Eve's heart, he needed to give his life to her. He needed to love her. In essence, God fixed Adam's aloneness by recreating him with a need to love someone, and then sending him on a treasure hunt to find that love relationship in the heart of his wife!

Now Adam had someone who was suitable and comparable to him—someone he could give his life to. Now he could live fully and completely in the image and likeness in which he was created. Notice the wording in Genesis 1:26: "Then God said, 'Let Us make man in Our image, according to Our likeness.' " In this most important Creation statement, God refers to himself in the plural. He is referring to himself as the Father, the Son, and the Holy Spirit. This is what we know as the Trinity—three Persons but one God.

The Trinity is the perfect relationship, the perfect family. There are three Persons, each uniquely individual and distinctly different, but so unified in purpose and commitment that they are one. To recognize that we were created in the image and likeness of the Trinity is to understand our deep need for relationship and family. As men and women created by God, we *need* to pour our lives into others through relationships and families in order to discover our purpose and be fulfilled in our lives.

When God created Adam and Eve, he created the potential to grow relationships, which have the potential to grow friendships, which have the potential to grow marriages, which can then grow families and eventually generations. Then he stepped back, took a look at his handiwork, and said, "Very good" (Genesis 1:31).

God Created Men and Women Alike Enough to Have Intimacy

By creating us male and female, God's goal is for husbands and wives to enjoy the relationship that is inherent in the Trinity: individuals totally equal in value, unique in personality and different in operation, but so committed to each other and unified in purpose that they are as one. Sometimes people think that because Adam was created first, man must be more important to God's purpose and plan. Not so.

Genesis 1:27 says, "So God created man in His own image; in the image of God He created him; male and female He created them." Both male and female were created in the image of God. Neither gender is more important; neither can fulfill God's purpose apart from the other.

In Eve, Adam found someone of equal value with whom he could pursue a relationship—and not just a casual relationship, because that would not fill the void of aloneness in his heart. He found someone with whom he could experience intimacy. Intimacy is the deepest desire of relationship, and it is only possible in an environment of equality and trust. I've heard intimacy defined as "in-to-me-see." As you grow in intimacy with another person, you see more and more into and through that person's life. You let that person into your heart and into your world, and he or she does the same. It is a very vulnerable place of both great risk and great reward. God created man and woman enough alike to make them comparable—to make them suitable for intimacy. Is intimacy a risk? Yes. But it's a risk worth taking.

Years ago I made a remarkable discovery. I had come up with a novel idea: I asked my oldest daughter, Angela, on a date. She was eight years old at the time. I'll never forget that night. As I came home from work and walked through the front door, I looked up. At the top of the spiral staircase in the entryway, a princess emerged. Dressed in all her finery and with an air of royalty, she began to descend the stairs in a very familiar way. I think every little girl practices this descent for that most important man in her life. It's called the "wedding walk." I was surprised to realize that at that moment, for Angela, *I* was that most important man.

So I put on my best suit, took my princess by the arm, and went off to enjoy the first of what would become a tradition in our family: the father-daughter date. As we sat by candlelight enjoying a quaint meal together, I thought, *How do you talk to an eight-year-old girl?* I had never really tried before! Clumsily I stumbled along, inquiring about her school, her friends, her likes and dislikes. Before long I was in tears, amazed by the discovery that this most amazing child with her own incredible world considered *me* to be the most important man in her life.

All children have their own worlds, and they are just as big and wonderful and important to them as our adult worlds are to us. In fact, every person has his or her own awesome world. Intimacy is how we share our worlds with one another. In an intimate relationship, two worlds converge—and the result is that both lives are bigger and richer for it. Such convergence between male and female worlds would be impossible if God had created men and women too different to connect with one another. Instead, he made us enough alike that we can, with effort and persistence, grow in intimacy and share our lives.

God Created Men and Women
Different Enough to Need One Another

We touched on this earlier, but the immediate result of God taking something out of the complete package called Adam was that man was no longer complete. Missing the ingredients God removed, man has been searching ever since for someone who has what he doesn't have—someone who is in some ways his "opposite." This explains why opposites attract; we all are looking for someone who can do what we can't do and be what we can't be. To live a complete and fulfilled life, we need each another. Because we are different *from* one another, we are necessary *to* one another.

God created male and female opposite in many ways. It's not just physiological differences. The way our brains function as we perceive and process our world are very different for male and female.

Psychologists have discovered that at about the third month

after conception, while in his mother's womb, a male baby undergoes what is known as a "testosterone wash." One of the results of this flood of male hormone is a restricting of the communication between the right and left hemispheres of the baby boy's cerebral cortex. Why is this important? Generally speaking, one side of the cerebral cortex deals with the outside, tactile world; the other processes the inside world of feelings and emotions. In little girls, communication takes place across the two hemispheres; in little boys, that communication is limited. This simple distinction accounts for a vast spectrum of differences between the average boy and the average girl.

As a bilateral thinker, a little girl will tend to relate what happens in her outside world to how it affects her feelings and emotions. This developing ability accounts for what we often call "women's intuition." Personally, I've learned to pay attention to my wife when she tells me she has a feeling about something. If I ask her, "How do you know?" she replies, "I don't know. I just know!" And she does! Females in general are quite astute when it comes to reading people. A little girl's brain is specially tuned to people and relationships; that's how God designed her.

A little boy, on the other hand, is likely to be more unilateral in his thinking—more focused on the outside, physical world than on his inner, emotional world. This explains, in part, why boys are often more physically oriented than girls. For example, boys will spend hours learning how to throw a ball to hit a moving target. Growing up in Canada, my favorite winter activity was throwing snowballs at passing cars. My sisters didn't understand it and the drivers didn't appreciate it, but I sure had fun!

This unilateral thinking also accounts for the generalization that boys can be more focused than girls. Have you ever noticed the difference between males and females watching TV? When a man is watching his sports game, he is oblivious to the world around him. The entire household can be in chaos, but he remains undisturbed and totally focused on the competition on the screen. A woman? You couldn't tie her to the couch. She is up in seconds, trying to make whatever is wrong right!

Women typically have well-developed relationship skills because they have spent their whole lives practicing and developing them. I know; I watched my three daughters practice mothering for years with their dolls. Everything in a little girl's life is about relationships. If you give a little girl two toy trucks to play with, the trucks will talk to each other. They will both have names. One will be a mommy truck, the other will be a daddy truck, and they will have baby trucks.

Men are not as skilled as women in the relationship department. That's because little boys, by and large, are all about *crash, boom, bang*. A boy doesn't want just a truck; he wants a *monster* truck—the bigger and noisier, the better. The purpose of everything in his world is to see how far he can throw it, how high he can climb up it, how fast he can slide down it, or how loud he can make it sound. If you give a little boy a doll to play with, he will try to rip the head off and play ball with it.

I taught this principle at a seminar one night, and the next night a mom came bounding up to me, excited to share her discovery. "Last night you talked about how boys and girls are different, and today I watched my children perfectly demonstrate it," she said. "We were shopping for groceries in the produce department. My little girl picked up two potatoes, and immediately she began her 'pretend game.' Both potatoes had names, and they began to talk to each other. When she finished, she put the two potatoes down and moved on to something else. Her little brother had been observing her, and he decided to pick up where she left off. He grabbed the two potatoes and began hitting them together with a *bam-bam* sound."

What this woman discovered was this: girls will be girls, and boys will be boys. Studies have shown that at four years of age, almost 100 percent of a little girl's sounds are words of communication, while about 60 percent of a little boy's sounds are just *sounds*—tires squealing, guns shooting, airplanes diving. In a room full of adult men and women, I love to have fun illustrating this difference. I simply ask the women to make a machine-gun sound. The men are always shocked to discover that most women can't—and that's only because they have never tried. In all their lives, it never crossed their minds to make a machine-gun sound! Most men, on the other hand, perfected the *rat-a-tat-tat* long before puberty.

I realize we're talking in generalities here. But for the most part, men are the way they are because God has hard-wired them to deal with the physical world. Genesis 2:15 says, "Then the LORD God took the man and put him in the garden of Eden to tend and keep it." God's original purpose for Adam was to "tend and keep" the physical world—to work, possess, and take care of the things he could see and touch. So God designed Adam—and every man after him—to be proficient at *doing* things. This explains why men, more than women, tend to define who they are by what they do. Have you ever noticed the first question a man asks when he meets another man? Invariably it's "What do you do?"

This also explains why men have a natural "conquering" mentality—and why so many wives wonder, *What happened to the romantic man my husband used to be before the wedding?* Romance is all about the pursuit. Before the wedding, a man is programmed to pursue and win his lady's heart. In order to accomplish this, he will do whatever it takes, even if it involves talking, sharing his feelings, and going shopping at the mall. After the wedding, though, he tends to target his conquering drive in new directions—good directions for the most part, such as building a home, a career, and a future for his family. Unfortunately, a wife usually interprets this change as a loss of romance in the marriage.

(I like to teach husbands that romance is the number-one expectation of every wife. She expects romance for a lifetime. Sometimes a husband needs to be informed that the goal was *not* the ring; the goal is to get to know and understand this amazing person he calls his wife. Romance is a treasure hunt, and the treasure is in her heart. Discovering it will take a lifetime!)

In general, females are hard-wired to be proficient at building relationships. God created Eve for the purpose of curing aloneness and completing a man, a family, and a community through relationships. This explains why women are not as interested in *what* others are doing as much as *how* they are doing. Their questions to one another are predominantly about relationships, because they find their identity in their relationships.

Women are also experts at communication. They know how to understand and share their feelings. Men, for the most part, are not so adept. As we've said, men are designed to conquer. Often, if they don't think they can win in a certain situation, they will choose not to even enter the arena. This is why so many wives complain about their husbands not wanting to talk. In the arena of open communication, a wife can usually come out victorious. Over time her husband begins to think, *Why bother?* Husbands and wives need to make sure the communication in their home doesn't become a competition. In such an arena, winning is really losing.

What's the bottom line here? In God's great, eternal plan, men and women are different on purpose—and these differences are the very things that make both male and female necessary. We need each other to live the complete, fulfilled lives that God intends for us. In general, the male is necessary for looking after the outside world, so the female can turn her attention to the more relational, inside world of home and family. The female is necessary for building relationships, families, and generations, so that man's aloneness can be removed and he can find meaning and purpose in all that he does.

The Perfect Learning Environment

As we mature in life, our goal must be to grow more and more complete. To do this, men and women need to grow in their understanding of one another. Males need to understand more about their inside world, and females need to understand more about their outside world. That's the beauty and ingenuity of God's plan: he created us to learn from one another. And what is his primary educational institution? The family. It is the perfect environment for learning healthy behaviors and skills for all future relationships.

In a family environment of unconditional acceptance and love, parents can train up their sons and daughters to be emotionally sound, complete adults who are fully capable of learning from one another, completing one another, and creating healthy families of their own. Sadly, this kind of healthy family environment is not all that common today. Dysfunctional homes, where children are left searching for acceptance and love—often in all the wrong places—are becoming more and more the norm. The result is that these hurting children become hurting adults who are not whole enough themselves to complete anyone else.

Men become husbands who don't know how to give themselves to their wives or discover the treasure in the female heart in a healthy way. They don't know how to be responsible with the outside world, protect their families, or channel their conquering mentality in positive directions. Women become wives who are so hurt that they put their treasure off limits. Since they've spent so much time feeling lost and alone themselves, they don't know how to use their God-given abilities to alleviate aloneness in others. They have no clue how to build healthy relationships. Together they compound and extend the problem by becoming the next generation of dysfunctional parents.

Is there an answer? How do we begin to heal the hurts and turn the tide? We begin with a desire and willingness between male and female to understand one another.

In a healthy family atmosphere, everyone is constantly learning from each other. In the best case scenario, there is both a mom and a dad. The family crosses genders and generations. This creates a safe haven where males can learn from females, females can learn from males, and generations can learn from each other. Real understanding can take place.

Of course, many homes don't fit this best case. Thankfully, in a single-parent home, a parent's relationship with God can make up the difference. Extended family—relatives, the local church, the community—can often help. The generational factor can be especially important for single-parent families, with grandparents providing safe cross-gender relationships for their grandsons and granddaughters. God always provides a way to make up for the missing pieces in our lives!

This is one of the most significant reasons why every parent should be vitally connected to a local church. Psalm 92:12–14 says, "But the godly will flourish like palm trees and grow strong like the cedars of Lebanon. For they are transplanted into the LORD's own house. They flourish in the courts of our God. Even in old age they will still produce fruit; they will remain vital and green" (NLT).

God promises that where he plants us, we will flourish. We personally know many incredible single parents who struggled because they felt so very alone, only to encounter a beautiful, giving, and loving company of people in the family of God. Once they were planted in a church, they and their families began to flourish.

Notice we didn't say the churches in which they were planted were perfect. No church is perfect, because it's always made up of imperfect people. But God has a home for everyone in his family. He wants each of us to be planted and committed to growth within a local church. In a healthy church environment, we can learn from others and they can learn from us.

Recently, while attending a meeting at a church in our city, Helen met an incredible young single mother who had been through many challenges in life. This woman had recently graduated from a program for young women dealing with difficult life issues, and she was now growing and flourishing in profound ways. When Helen asked about her family, the young woman responded with a beautiful, confident smile, "I have no family—no one. This church is my family, and they are raising me." What a blessing to know that God our Father will provide for any lack in our lives! We are never left destitute when we are connected to God and his amazing family.

Yes, there are differences between boys and girls. And yes, along with those differences come unique challenges, as we seek to raise our sons and daughters to become healthy, mature, and loving adults. But for every challenge that we face, we can rest assured that God provides the answer. As moms and dads in two-parent homes and even single-parent homes, we need only to look to our heavenly Father. We can trust him to guide and provide.

Part 1

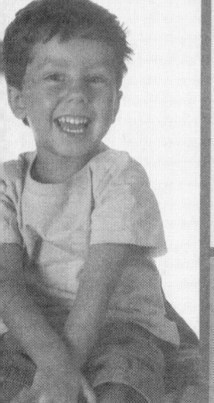

What *Moms* Need to Know about *Sons*

A mother's desire to understand her son can equip her with the power to influence his life for good, thereby influencing his family, and his family's family, and all the generations to come.

—John Burns

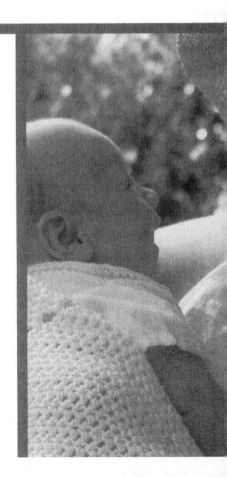

chapter

1

It's a Boy!

The announcement, "It's a boy!" is welcomed by every new mother with excitement, thanksgiving—and trepidation. It signifies the beginning of a great adventure, one that includes snakes, spiders, snails, bumps, scrapes, dirty hands, and muddy shoes. It is the beginning of what may be the most challenging job a human being could ever take on: raising a boy.

Something very amazing happens to a woman when she becomes the mother of a son. I have three daughters, and they are all mothers now. One of them has a son; and since his birth, I have

3

witnessed in her an intense desire to figure out why males do what they do—not to judge or compare him to the female of the species, but simply to understand why he's different.

If only every mother of a newborn baby boy realized how important she was! W. R. Wallace, a nineteenth-century poet, wrote, "The hand that rocks the cradle is the hand that rules the world." He was describing the power of influence. Mothers have tremendous influence; and according to leadership expert John Maxwell, that makes them leaders.[1] Mothers are leaders because they literally influence generations. They can change the world—for good or for bad. What makes the difference? Understanding. Understanding is the beginning of positive influence. A mother's desire to understand her son can equip her with the power to influence his life for good, thereby influencing his family, and his family's family, and all the generations to come.

> Mothers are leaders because they literally influence generations.

Are you a mother who wants to understand her son? He may be two months old, or two years, or twelve, or twenty. It's never too early—or too late—to start the understanding process. Hopefully the next few chapters will open your eyes, your mind, and your heart to see your son in a new, more complete light. As you turn the page, remember: God made you this little boy's mom on purpose!

chapter

2

The Challenge

Every little boy grows up full of dreams—dreams of being the hero, scoring the winning goal, flying the airplane, driving the racecar, riding the horse, catching the lion, saving the day. He looks forward to manhood with wide-open, starry eyes, full of anticipation, expecting the future to be bigger than life itself. Intuitively, he relishes the challenges ahead. After all, heroes and champions are defined only by the challenges they overcome. To a boy, life is all about challenge!

Recently we took some out-of-town guests

7

to see Vancouver's famous Queen Elizabeth Park. Our guests love flowers, so we knew they'd enjoy strolling through this natural rock quarry filled with stunning gardens. I brought my five-year-old grandson along, and I could read the look on his face. As everyone else *ooh*ed and *aah*ed over the amazing colors and arrangements of the gardens, his eyes were scaling up the rock cliff, and I knew exactly what was going through his mind. "No, you can't climb up there," I said. He didn't want to look at flower beds; he wanted to take on a challenge!

I could relate. When I was a child, every day seemed to hold a new adventure—catching snakes, grasshoppers, or bumblebees; building forts in the trees or dams in the puddles; throwing perfectly packed snowballs at moving targets. Life was full of challenges, and I wanted to meet them head on. I was a typical boy—just like my grandson.

You see, God purposely designed boys to be challengers. They seemingly have no fear. They climb first and consider how to get down later. (I remember more than once getting stuck in a high place, not realizing that the way up was a lot easier than the way down!) As parents, we need to celebrate this aggressive aspect of our sons' God-given nature.

Let's be clear though. Aggressive behavior is not the same as violent behavior. With aggressive behavior, you challenge yourself and others to rise to new heights of achievement. The goal is to be better by increasing performance. With violent behavior, however, you seek to hurt others and damage their property. The goal is to be better by pulling others down.

> The goal is to be better by increasing performance.

Boys are naturally aggressive. Have you ever noticed how little boys bond? They wrestle. They challenge each other physically. This is good; we need to allow them to exercise aggressiveness. At the same time, we need to teach them how to harness that aggressiveness so that it never crosses over into violence. God did not create males to be violent!

Tied to a boy's natural aggression is the equally natural phenomenon of male competitiveness. Boys and even grown men tend to make everything into a competition. For example, have you noticed the way males drive? This is still one of the biggest contentions in my marriage. Helen cannot understand why I'm always trying to pass the person next to me. When we approach a multilane intersection, why do I always count the cars, analyze the

9

drivers of those cars, and choose the lane that will be the fastest? Why don't I just relax and enjoy the trip? Because I'm male!

Aggression and competitiveness are built into the male soul. They're necessary qualities that help men fulfill God's original statement about man: "Let them have dominion" (Genesis 1:26). It was part of Adam's God-given nature to want to conquer and have dominion; it's been part of every man's nature ever since. Males have a drive to conquer. They're built to be aggressive and competitive. These are positive capacities—as long as they're harnessed appropriately and aimed in the right direction.

Playing with Fire

Learning to harness aggression can be difficult. But that's not the greatest challenge that boys face in our modern world. No, the greatest challenge begins around the age of puberty and continues long into adulthood. It's mastering the male sex drive.

Ever since God took something out of Adam, males have been searching for what's missing from their lives. Men are on a treasure hunt—and God has packaged this treasure in a "Do Not Touch" container. First Corinthians 7:1 says, "Now concerning the things of which you wrote to me: It is good for a man not to touch a woman." This warning is directed at unmarried men. The English word *touch* comes from the Greek word *haptoo*, which can be translated "to kindle, set on fire."[1] In other words, when a man touches a woman, he's playing with fire.

Why? Because God created men to be very physically oriented. They tend to discover the world through their five senses. As a result, when a male experiences physical stimulation, it's as if a match has been struck. The male hormone, testosterone, is released, and huge cardiovascular changes begin to take place. The body shifts blood from the brain to other organs to prepare for sexual involvement.

In other words, when the male sex drive is activated, it literally drains the brain! A single male who puts his hand in the fire loses the capacity to think straight. He doesn't notice he's getting burned until it's too late.

A number of years ago I happened upon some information about the male sex drive that has captivated me and many people with whom I've shared it—especially mothers with sons. My wife, Helen, leads a wonderful women's ministry that meets at our church every Tuesday morning. One Tuesday, however, she found herself double-booked. She had inadvertently agreed to teach at another ministry during the same time period. She pleaded with me for help. "Here, just teach my notes," she said, handing me her papers and ushering me off to the church.

Little did I know that I was being launched into a new journey of discovery—and a new ministry of helping moms understand their sons.

I stood before that room full of moms, poring silently over my wife's notes. They were obviously written from a woman to women. *There is no way I can teach this,* I thought. Fishing for an alternative, I asked if anyone had a question. A single mom raised her hand.

"I have a son who's thirteen," she said. "I think I know what he's doing behind closed doors, but what should I do about it?"

I have never spoken to such a captive audience. As I began to answer, you could have heard a pin drop in that room. These moms were anxious to understand their sons. I was amazed at how attentive they were.

Not so coincidentally (God knew I would be speaking to those women that Tuesday), I had just finished reading *The Sexual Man* by Christian psychologist Archibald Hart.[2] This interesting book gave me some key points to help explain the sexual dilemma boys and men face in our society today. As I shared my understanding of this vital but mostly neglected topic (neglected, at least, from the Christian point of view), I was astounded at the impact my words had on the moms in the room. Eventually I developed a seminar on the subject of male sexuality called "From Adolescence to the Altar." I've had the privilege of sharing this message with moms and other groups around the world, and everywhere I go I get the same passionate and attentive reception.

I am indebted to Dr. Hart. When I first read *The Sexual Man*, it was as if a light bulb went off in my head. The book unlocked for me a greater understanding of male sexuality and the impact of our overtly sexual society on the attitudes and development of our boys and young men. It was this new understanding that helped me answer the single mom's question that Tuesday and many more questions since.

> It was this new understanding that helped me answer the single mom's question that Tuesday . . .

The Sexual Challenge

Dr. Hart's book and my own studies have convinced me that the greatest addiction in our society today is immoral sex. The victims are our sons (and daughters). The coconspirators are ignorance and silence. The taskmasters, as in every addiction, are guilt and shame. How can our boys avoid this addiction, or escape it if caught? Only through understanding—the result of much communication with parents and other caring adults.

Let me describe the sexual challenge that society presents our young males today, as well as some of the key factors that make this challenge so significant.

The Gap between Physical and Emotional Development

In the nineteenth century, the average age for a young person to hit puberty was seventeen. That was also the age he or she was considered mature enough to marry. How convenient! Today, the average age for the beginning of puberty is twelve, with some children starting these critical hormonal changes as young as nine. And what is the average age that a modern young person gets married for the first time? For a woman, it's twenty-five. For a man, it's twenty-eight![3]

What is the reason for this colossal shift? I don't have all the answers. But I do believe that society's increase in seductive, sensual media has much to do with it. These factors help create a substantial gap between male physical and emotional development—and a substantial challenge for boys growing up in the twenty-first century.

As we noted earlier, testosterone is the male hormone. Following the onset of puberty, it is released in large doses in a male's body in response to sexual stimulation. Understand, a hormone is a drug—an endogenous ("self-made") drug. When a male is sexually stimulated, it is like putting a tourniquet around his arm, pumping up his veins, and injecting him with a syringe full of testosterone.

As a drug, testosterone is powerful. It's similar to adrenaline—the hormone that allows little old ladies to pick up cars or jump high fences in emergency situations. Like adrenaline, testosterone is a tremendous stimulant. It increases a person's heart rate, blood pressure, and body temperature, and stimulates the central and peripheral nervous systems. In the vernacular of drugs, we might classify it as an "upper."

Here's the typical scenario: Around twelve years of age, a growing boy discovers what makes him feel good. This happens as a result of natural curiosity and the fact that God created males with external and very accessible genitalia. The boy will either wake up

This is the beginning of the negative cycle of addiction.

to a "wet dream," or he will experience a climax after stimulating himself. Usually he has not been forewarned about his body's response, so the experience is surprising and even frightening. When this reaction is coupled with the uncomfortable silence of society in general and Mom and Dad in particular, the boy evaluates the experience as "bad," and he feels guilty. This is the beginning of the negative cycle of addiction.

Every addiction works the same way. First you do something that makes you feel bad. In response, you judge yourself as bad. "As [a man] thinks in his heart, so is he," Solomon said in Proverbs 23:7. So what happens when you feel bad about yourself? You do more of the "bad thing" that made you feel bad in the first place. After all, bad people do bad things, right? Unfortunately, the more you do, the worse you feel—which makes you do the "bad thing" even more. Can you see how easily the downward spiral of addiction begins, and why it spins so quickly out of control?

An immoral sex addiction is like a drug addiction. The only difference is that a person's own body manufactures the drug in response to real or perceived stimuli. A testosterone addict is not enslaved to the drug dealer. He is enslaved to the stimuli dealer.

The guilt that results not only perpetuates the negative behavior of addiction, it also protects it. When you feel guilty about something, you naturally hide it. This is why the whole topic of male sexuality is so misunderstood. Men don't readily talk about their sexuality. The topic is hidden under a cloud of guilt, and boys suffer as a result. Their early feelings of sexual desire are interpreted as evil, when actually they are common to all males and not evil in and of themselves. Communication is critical if boys and young men are going to properly understand their sexuality and ultimately use it for its God-given purpose.

The Denial of Male Emotion

In today's macho society, boys are taught to deny, hide, and repress their emotions. After all, "real men" don't have feelings. They never cry. They're like the robot-men made popular by Hollywood: They're indestructible machines. Feelings don't affect them; they bounce off like bullets off of Superman's chest. Men are hard and strong. Impenetrable fortresses. They don't talk about feelings. Feelings and emotions are female. Muscle is male!

I remember a time when I was very young, and I had hurt

myself. I naturally began to cry. Immediately I was scolded, "Boys don't cry. Don't be a sissy! Only girls cry!" That was the last time I cried—not for pain, not for a sad movie, not even for a funeral. I worked hard to toughen myself to the emotions that I believed would betray my masculinity. I taught myself how to disengage my feelings.

This is a huge component of the sexual challenge in our society today. By teaching boys to repress their emotions, society has trained them to disconnect the physical feelings of sexual stimulation from the heart-feelings of emotion. This is why most husbands would—however reluctantly—respond yes if asked, "Is it possible for a man to enjoy sex with a woman other than his wife?" Most wives, on the other hand, would answer no to the corresponding question, "Is it possible for a woman to enjoy sex with a man other than her husband?" Women correctly connect the physical feelings of sexual stimulation with the emotional feelings of love. Men don't always make that same connection.

The Repression of Male Sensuality

A similar issue is the repression of male sensuality. In today's society, boys learn how *not* to be affectionate and sensitive. The outcome is that when they grow up, they are unable to fulfill their wives' greatest need, which is for affection (not just sex). As with love, their feelings of affection are disconnected from their feelings of sexual stimulation.

From an early age, boys discover that it's not cool to be seen holding hands with Mom. They learn that being touchy-feely is not macho; it's a practice that will get them shunned by their peers. It may even earn them the nickname Momma's Boy. They must be tough to survive. If a mother raises her son to be too tender and sensitive, he may come home from school with a black eye. The young male social world can be so cruel!

The Perversion of Male Ego

God has assigned men the responsibility of guarding and protecting their families. To help them fulfill this protective and provisionary role, he has given them their male ego as a source of strength. A healthy ego in a man is a good thing! Unfortunately, society has perverted the male ego, evolving it into an unhealthy machismo.

Machismo is what pits men against women in the arena of sex. It says, "The more macho a man is, the more women he can conquer sexually." It correlates male ego with sexual conquest. As a

19

result, the very thing that should empower men to protect women is perverted to encourage men to victimize women!

The Seduction of Modern Society

Who can deny this last factor? What was considered pornography in the 1950s is deemed perfectly normal on the cover of almost any of today's popular magazines. In movies, music, and media in general, sex is everywhere. Unfortunately, this proliferation of sexually seductive media over the past fifty or sixty years has compounded the challenge of raising mentally, emotionally, and socially healthy boys—and there's no slowdown in sight. In fact, the availability of sexually stimulating content continues to skyrocket, along with the explosion of communications technology.

> In movies, music, and media in general, sex is everywhere.

A few years ago, I had a very educational encounter while in flight from Vancouver to Auckland, New Zealand, where I was scheduled to speak at the amazing Parachute Festival (a youth music festival) on the topic of sexuality. I settled into my seat and began the usual friendly banter with the man seated next to me. We discovered an exciting common interest. We were both involved in television production. I was on the side of speaking into the camera, and he was on the side of producing the equipment that made it all happen.

I explained that my goal was to reach and help as many people as possible with positive programming. Helen and I had been producing our own program, *Family Success*, for years, and it was airing in many nations around the world. Our constant challenge was to find more stations that would agree to air our show. For some time I had been wondering if the Internet might be the answer. Certainly, if we could broadcast over the Internet, anyone anywhere could access the program on their computer.

"How long before we can broadcast worldwide over the Internet?" I asked the broadcast executive.

"Oh, it will be a long time still," he responded.

"But why? All the technology is already available."

His answer shocked me. "There's no room. Over 90 percent of the bandwidth is presently hogged by adult entertainment," he said.

This is a wake-up call for parents. A dangerous multibillion-dollar industry is targeting our sons. It is overtaking virtually every media outlet. It is monopolizing the Internet. Its poisonous fingers are reaching out not so much to "bad boys" as to normal, curious, uninformed boys who can't help the fact that they live in a society inundated with sexual stimuli.

What's the Battle Plan?

Understand, it's normal for a boy to be curious, and it's normal for his body to react with sexual sensations to sexual stimuli. The question is, in our current social climate, how is he going to learn how to master his sex drive rather than allow it to master him? How is he going to grow up to become a mature, loving, affectionate husband with a healthy ego and a healthy, God-given drive to protect and provide for his wife and children?

> Our sons are in a battle, and they cannot fight it without our help.

Our sons are in a battle, and they cannot fight it without our help. They need us—parents and churches and concerned friends who will teach them and fight for them and guard them physically, spiritually, mentally, and emotionally. Communication is critical. The worst thing we can do is keep our sons uninformed and thus unprepared to successfully navigate the challenge of their boyhood years.

Thankfully, for every challenge, there is a God-given answer.

CHAPTER 2: THE CHALLENGE

As parents and concerned adults, it's our duty to wage the battle against sexual immorality on many fronts. Our sons, however, can find their answer much closer to home.

Her name is Mom.

chapter 3

Moms Are the Answer

When a little boy falls down and scrapes his knee, who does he run to? When he is sad and needs comfort, where does he go? When he fails and needs encouragement, who does he want to see? His mom, of course.

Moms are warm, loving, encouraging, soft, and strong. Moms are miraculous. Moms are heroes. Moms are the answer for every son.

Every young boy has an inexplicable connection to his mom. She is different from everyone else in his life. In fact, for a boy, there are three species of human beings: male, female, and

Mom. If asked for a one-word description of his mom, a young boy is most likely to respond, "Beautiful." This revelation comes long before he understands the definition of *beauty* according to society's shallow standard. A little boy intuitively understands Proverbs 31:30: "Charm is deceitful and beauty is passing, but a woman who fears the LORD, she shall be praised." He falls in love with the real beauty in his mother—not the outer package, but the treasure in her heart.

Isn't it marvelous how God has created us so different and yet so interdependent? Moms and sons are as different as can be, and yet their relationship is special. In fact, it's absolutely vital! Have you ever seen a big, burly football player being interviewed on television? Typically, he sees the camera, waves, and shouts, "Hi, Mom!" I have never heard, "Hi, Dad!"

Why is Mom every boy's hero? Heroes by nature are different from us. They have something we don't have, or they do something we can't do. Moms have capabilities that sons don't have, and they do things that sons can't do. As a result, Mom is a superheroine who holds a powerful position in her son's life. She has a unique, God-given ability to influence her son's development in a vital and necessary way.

A dad plays a powerful role in raising his son, but it's a different role. A boy wants to be strong and successful for his father. He wants to show him how much he is growing up to be like him. For this reason, it is much harder for a boy to open up and be vulnerable with his dad. A boy looks up to Dad as a role model. He looks to Mom for understanding and emotional support.

Several years ago I wrote a book called *The Miracle in a Daddy's Hug*. Afterwards, Helen wrote *The Miracle in a Mother's Hug*. For a son, there is definitely a miracle in both. With his dad's arms wrapped around him, a son feels strong, safe, and secure. With his mom's arms wrapped around him, he feels loved, lovable, and understood. A great relationship with Dad is critical for many aspects of his development, including a healthy identity and sense of self-worth. But ultimately it's the mother-son relationship that is the key to his preparation for healthy future relationships.

As we said in the last chapter, our society pushes boys to repress their emotions, hide their sensitivities, and avoid showing affection. It encourages them to view their sexuality as an instrument of ego and conquest and to view women as objects of exploitation and lust. The result is nothing short of disastrous. Young males with poor communication skills pursue unhealthy relationships with females. Emotionally immature, they're totally unprepared to enter into a loving, mature relationship with a woman. They have no idea how a woman thinks and feels or how to meet the unique needs of a wife. They end up with empty marriages, broken vows, and hurting children who grow up with the same struggles and deficiencies as their parents—which then get passed on to the next generation.

> A mother's heart is a child's first classroom.

It doesn't have to be this way. Society pushes hard, and its message is loud. But a wise and loving mom can exert more influence. Your patient and discerning voice can rise above the din! As a mom, you have the unique ability to personally counter every one of society's arguments in your son's heart and mind through your words, actions, and example.

Last May I sat down to develop a Mother's Day message for my church. As I pondered what to share with the congregation, I was keenly aware that I didn't get to where I was in life on my own. My life was the sum total of what I had learned and copied from other people—and especially from my mom.

A mother's heart is a child's first classroom. I remember coming home from school and finding Mom doing the ironing, or maybe preparing something for dinner. I would grab a bite to eat, pull up a chair, and unload a head-full of questions. I would ask every kind of question conceivable. Nothing was off limits. Mom and I would talk about God, heaven, death, miracles, suffering, poverty, and world crises. We could talk about anything and everything. I look back now and understand that much of my world-view was framed in those discussions.

Moms Teach Their Sons to Communicate

One thing that boys need to learn is how to communicate from the heart. One of the most frequent complaints that Helen and I hear from wives—no matter where we are around the globe—is, "My husband won't talk to me." These wives aren't referring to conversations about the latest sports game or business deal. They are referring to their husbands' ineptitude at sharing feelings. Most men never stop to think about what they're feeling. They just *do*. As a result, they tend to be out of touch with their feelings and inexperienced at discussing them.

Remember how, back in the Garden of Eden, God took something out of the male and used it to create the female? (Since then,

29

men have been looking for what's missing in themselves.) I'm convinced that males in general lack the ability to communicate feelings because this skill was part of the inventory that God removed from Adam to create Eve. The Catch-22 is that males need to know how to communicate in order to discover the treasure that is inside a woman. Communication is the key that unlocks the door to an intimate husband-wife relationship.

From the beginning, God created women with the emotional makeup necessary for successful communication. This is why girls are generally better at building relationships than boys. Life is all about relationships—and relationships are developed through communication. In this department, most males need help. But where is a boy going to learn effective communication skills? From Mom—she is the answer.

Recently I was listening to a great mom who raised three magnificent, healthy boys. She was reminiscing over some of the golden moments in her sons' development. She said that from early childhood on, she would tuck them into bed and stay there talking until she was satisfactorily updated on the matters of their hearts. Sometimes the boys didn't want to open up; but, "Moms have the right to pry," she explained with a smile. She would ask whatever questions were necessary to discover what was going on in each of her son's hearts and lives. She didn't want them going to sleep holding anything inside.

It is important for your son to have someone safe to share his heart with. You are safe, because you have your son's best interests at heart. A boy who grows up not having this healthy outlet for sharing his thoughts and feelings is much more susceptible to unhealthy friendships and manipulative motives. Not all girls will have your son's best interests at heart! There are some young women who could potentially hurt your young man if he is unskilled at communication and unprepared for a relationship. As his mom, you are the best defense against such manipulation.

Moms Protect Their Sons' Emotions

A girl who has not had her needs met in a healthy family with a healthy dad can grow up to be emotionally unhealthy. (To understand this concept more, please read Helen's half of this book, *What Dads Need to Know about Daughters*.) She has what my friend Nancy Alcorn, founder of Mercy Ministries, calls a daddy vacuum—a vacuum in her life that she may try to fill with unhealthy things. Unfortunately, actions that are motivated by a hurting heart usually

31

hurt others. Many a young man has paid the price for a little girl's daddy vacuum.

A positive relationship with Mom is a son's first line of protection. Consider this scenario: A young man has been raised by a competent, informed, loving mother. Since childhood he has consistently spent countless hours with Mom, being instructed in relationships and learning the art of communication. Mom has always tucked him into bed at night and stayed to talk. She has answered his questions—and asked questions of her own—in the kitchen, around the dinner table, and in the car on the way to soccer practices and baseball games. Her goal has been to understand her son's heart and teach him to understand and communicate his feelings. Their relationship has been warm, loving, and intimate.

> A positive relationship with Mom is a son's first line of protection.

This young man has a huge advantage as he moves forward in his life and his relationships. Why? Because all males were created with needs. Think back to our analysis of God fixing the aloneness in Adam. The substance that God took out of man created and defined his need; then God took this very substance and created woman. As a result, the key quality that characterizes a woman is also what men need: the desire and ability to develop deep, intimate, heartfelt relationships.

Willard Harley, in his classic book *His Needs, Her Needs,* uses the metaphor of a bank account to explain how we keep the emotional feelings of love alive in our intimate relationships. He says that when a male and female meet each other's needs, they make deposits into one another's emotional bank accounts. A mom who meets her son's need to relate to a female on a deep level is making regular deposits into his emotional bank account. Within the safety of his own home, he experiences the positive release of good feelings that comes from having an important need met. Later, when he meets a young woman and develops a close relationship with her, he is not surprised by the surge of positive emotions he feels. Because he has had a healthy mother-son relationship, he is equipped to deal with his feelings; he's not knocked off his feet by them.

A Struggle to Communicate

Now consider the counter-scenario. A young man grows up without being equipped by his mother to understand and communicate his feelings. He is typically male—very focused on his *doings* and on conquering his outside world, but out of touch with his inner world of emotions and feelings. His lack of emotional training leaves him emotionally immature. Later in life, when he wants to build a relationship with a woman, he has two serious challenges. The first is that he lacks confidence in talking to females; he doesn't know how to speak their language.

This kind of relational hurt is called "heartache," and heartache is the worst ache of all.

I remember how afraid I was to talk to girls when I was young. In my case, the problem wasn't a lack of equipping by Mom, but rather an intense struggle with stuttering. The result, however, was the same. I'm like a lot of men; when a male lacks confidence in an area, he tends to either avoid it, pouring himself into other areas where he is more confident; or he shoves ahead like a bull in a china shop, with a very good chance of hurting the other person involved (and himself too). This kind of relational hurt is called "heartache," and heartache is the worst ache of all.

A common observation from wives complaining about silent husbands is that something changed after the wedding. During the courting season, a wife will say, her husband had no problem opening up and sharing his heart; but once they were married, his conversation dried up. I mentioned this in an earlier chapter, but let me explain what I think happens: before the wedding, the man has his conquering sights trained on winning the heart of his lady. This requires communication, so he applies himself to the task. After the wedding, however, he refocuses his sights on conquering other aspects of their future together. His communication technique returns to autopilot—that is, he falls back into the poor communication habits he learned growing up.

An Unfamiliar Rush

The second challenge for an unprepared young man goes back to the bank-account idea. Because of the deficiency in his relationship with his mother, he is not familiar with the rush that comes from a woman making deposits in his emotional bank account. Such an explosion of good emotions is entirely unfamiliar. As a result, when he meets a girl who is able to pry open his heart and he experiences how rewarding it is to share his feelings, he becomes a sitting duck for manipulation and heartache.

I like to coach young people who are dating and building new relationships to use wisdom. The best chaperone is always wisdom! I encourage them to keep their brains engaged at all times, so that the choices they make come from wisdom, not emotion. Unfortunately, following this advice is a much greater challenge for young men who are emotionally immature. Engulfed in a fog of raging hormones and unfamiliar feelings, they often make unwise choices, resulting in painful scars they may carry for the rest of their lives.

Moms Teach Their Sons Affection

Another thing that boys need to learn is how to show affection. In *His Needs, Her Needs*, Willard Harley identifies affection as a woman's number one need.[1] Many men don't understand this aspect of womanhood. I've heard it explained that to a woman, affection is "hug, period," whereas to a man, it's "hug, comma." A wife needs her husband to hold her affectionately because of who she is, not because of the sexual gratification he expects to receive. The question is, where can a normal, red-blooded young male learn to be affectionate without crossing over the sexual line? From Mom.

For years I have espoused the belief that girls and boys can't be "just friends," due to the physiological factors involved in such relationships. I tell young people that every healthy male-female relationship progresses, and the potential for physical involvement increases with that progression. Therefore, to build a special friendship with someone of the opposite sex is to set yourself on a road that most likely will lead to physical involvement. Unless the person is a potential marriage partner, you shouldn't get on the road! I am not saying that boys and girls can't have a number of people they call friends, including some who are of the opposite sex. I am saying that it's not wise to have an exclusive friend who is of the opposite sex, unless you are considering marriage.

> I am saying that it's not wise to have an exclusive friend who is of the opposite sex, unless you are considering marriage.

For a boy, there is only one exception to this rule: Mom! Mom is safe. As a mother, you can build a friendship with your son without any of the typical male/female hormonal interference. This makes you the perfect teacher. Not only can you instruct your son on how to treat a woman with affection, but you can also help him understand how a woman thinks and feels. You can educate him on how to respect all women and treat them with dignity. You can be your son's communications coach—as well as his model for what to look for in a prospective wife.

Unfortunately, in our society too many men think of women as objects to be exploited for their pleasure. Somehow these men have never connected the concept of *women* to *real people with real feelings*. Interestingly, these same macho men would never allow anyone to think of their mothers in the way they think of other women. Obviously, it has not dawned on them that Mom is a female!

In some societies—and in some men's hearts—motherhood is almost worshiped. The mother holds the place of highest influence in her son's life, and she continues to wield that influence into his adult years, even after he is married. This kind of mothering isn't healthy, however—not for the son, his wife, his family, or society in general. A healthy husband loves and honors his mother but regards his wife as the most important and influential woman in his life. Unfortunately, some men never move beyond the "Mom-as-a-third-species" concept, and their wives suffer for it.

> In some societies—and in some men's hearts—motherhood is almost worshiped.

Moms Influence Generations

A wise mom will make sure that her relationship with her son transitions into friendship as he grows up. When children are small, they are totally dependent on their parents. As they mature into adulthood, however, they become more and more independent. A healthy parent-child relationship reflects this change and progressively transitions from a base of total dependency to one of friendship. A mom who tries to hang on too long in a controlling manner usually pays the price of rebellion in her adolescent or young adult son. He must have the opportunity, from a position of independence, to *choose* friendship with his mom (and dad); otherwise, it's not really friendship at all.

Proverbs 13:20 says, "He who walks with wise men will be wise, but the companion of fools will be destroyed." Proverbs 24:6 adds, "In a multitude of counselors there is safety." What do these verses have to do with mothers and sons? Consider two points. First, on a functional level, our counselors are most often our friends; they are the ones we go to for advice in life. Second, the people our grown children choose to associate with as friends and counselors will make the difference between success and failure in their lives. This means that if we as parents want to be among the

39

companions and counselors our kids turn to—if we want to help them be successful adults who make wise choices—we must be their friends first.

Personally, I want my grown children to *want* to spend time with Helen and me because of friendship. I want them to value the wisdom we can share with them and seek us out. This isn't something that automatically happens, just because we're their parents. It happens because we're their friends.

From the moment your son gets married, his wife must have first place in his life. But if you, as a mom, are also a friend, you can still be a tremendous blessing to him and his family. Through friendship, you can have a gentle, loving influence that is invited, not forced. The result is a healthy son with a healthy marriage—and a healthy extended family that spans generations.

4

Boys Will Be Men

What mother with sons hasn't thrown up her hands in exasperation, declaring, "Boys will be boys"? She's right—boys *will* be boys. But that should be a positive statement! Unfortunately, those four words are often spoken in a negative way to vent frustration over a son's perceived lack of maturity and development. Personally, I believe we should celebrate boys being boys. We should recognize and understand the differences between boys and girls and believe that God did a good thing in creating male and female just the way they are.

Boys who are celebrated become healthier

41

men. They go forward faster and stronger with their God-given dream to change the world. When we focus on the good things we see in our sons, we get more of those good things. The old adage is true: what you see is what you get. Choose to see the man in your boy!

I still remember what it felt like when I was a boy and someone celebrated my strengths. It was as if they had just added jet fuel to

> When we focus on the good things we see in our sons, we get more of those good things.

my motivation. Once my mother praised me for being smart with numbers like my dad and my granddad. Suddenly math became my favorite subject!

As a child I was mesmerized watching my Uncle Robert play the accordion. I especially liked hearing the polkas. So, at about twelve years old, I began accordion lessons. Like most kids taking lessons on a musical instrument, I had fun at first; but after about two months, the novelty wore off, and practice became very dry and laborious. Everything changed, though, when I was finally good enough to play a polka. My mom and dad loved that first polka, and they bragged that I sounded like Uncle Robert. I'm sure I beamed inside and out. For the next several years, I practiced up to four hours a day, and eventually I became a fairly accomplished accordion player. (I know that most people don't think accordion music is cool, but that's because they've lived sheltered lives.)

Here's my point: a huge factor in determining who we become in life is the vision that others speak into our lives. The most potent words come from the most important people—and as we said in the last chapter, no one is more important to a boy than Mom. As a mother sees and praises the character of the man in her son, she fuels his desire to become that man of character.

Where Are All the Good Men?

Every mother who is raising a son is actually raising a man. The seeds of male greatness, strength, valor, and wisdom—qualities that our world desperately needs in its men—are on the inside of our boys. Yet, as Helen and I travel extensively speaking on relationships, we're amazed at how often we're confronted with the question, "Where are all the good men?" According to many women, there is a global drought of good, strong men with whom they can forge healthy, satisfying, long-term relationships.

The good news is, there are more than enough good men in seed form on Planet Earth. They are called boys. Like every seed, these seeds require the right soil to grow and flourish. The family and community that surround a boy is the soil in which he is planted. It is made up of many important people—male and female, young and old, in the home and outside it—playing many important roles in his upbringing. Mom, of course, is at the top of the list.

A mother's perspective is a valuable resource to her son. She intuitively knows what a woman needs in a real man. Young girls may be impressed with a boy's outer appearance and abilities, but a mom is focused more on her son's inner character and strengths. She understands and values character. She loves her son and envisions him becoming what this world really needs in a man.

> A mother's perspective is a valuable resource to her son.

This vision of the man in her son is a powerful, creative force. Jesus said, "A good man out of the good treasure of his heart brings forth good things" (Matthew 12:35). Our good treasure is the vision we see of the future. Out of this vision, we actually bring forth the future. In fact, the vision of the future that we see with our hearts is more powerful than the vision of the present that we see with our eyes. When a mother's heart envisions her son's future, it becomes the womb from which she births the man her son will become.

Like physical birth, however, this birthing process is hard work—especially when a boy is not acting like the man his mom believes he will become. The physical labor a mother goes through to birth her baby boy is just the beginning. Afterward comes the mental and spiritual labor that is necessary to birth the man inside the boy. As a mother fights to stay focused on seeing and encouraging her son's inner man, she actually gives birth to that man.

Building a Son's Male Ego

As we've noted before, God created and equipped men to deal with the outside world. They are supposed to be the providers and protectors of their families. This responsibility requires inner strength—that is, a healthy male ego. A mom is in the best position and has the best opportunity to build this healthy ego into her son's life.

One of the greatest needs of a husband is a wife who is his cheerleader. Ephesians 5:33 in the Amplified Bible says, "Let the wife see that she respects and reverences her husband [that she notices him, regards him, honors him, prefers him, venerates, and esteems him; and that she defers to him, praises him, and loves and admires him exceedingly]." If that verse sounds a little overboard to you, notice that God repeats the message in 1 Peter 3:2. Speaking to wives, he says, ". . . together with your reverence [for your husband; you are to feel for him all that reverence includes: to respect, defer to, revere him—to honor, esteem, appreciate, prize, and, in the human sense, to adore him, that is, to admire, praise, be devoted to, deeply love, and enjoy your husband]."

Of course, my wife thinks these are my favorite Bible verses. That's beside the point. Clearly, God is in favor of women encouraging a healthy ego in their men. I know how important my wife's encouragement is to me. After I have preached on a Sunday, many people may compliment me, but what my wife says has the most impact. She is the most important female—the most important person—in my life.

> Males are all about doing, and praise is the fuel for their doing.

Interestingly, the most important words that a husband can say to his wife, or a father can say to his daughter, is "I love you," followed with an explanation of why.

46

The same is not true for a husband or son. The most important words that a wife can say to her husband, or a mother can say to her son, is, "I'm proud of you," followed with an explanation. Males are all about doing, and praise is the fuel for their doing.

Before a boy grows up, gets married, and has a wife, his mom is his best cheerleader. When you love, adore, revere, respect, and admire your son, you teach him how to be loved by a woman in the same way. You fuel his self-esteem and sense of self-worth and set a standard for his future. As a result, he becomes a strong, secure young man who doesn't have to resort to anger, control, or manipulation to build his future. Instead, he is able to attract strong, secure relationships, and one day choose a wife who compliments his strengths.

Confirming a Son's Masculinity

As a mom, you can teach your son a lot about masculinity—not machismo, but true masculine character based on a healthy (not overblown) male ego. One of the best ways you can do this is by talking to your son about the men you love and why you love them. By doing this, you are actually seeding your son's heart with these very characteristics. When my mom told me stories about the wisdom of her father, I would dream about becoming a man of wisdom. When she praised my dad's work ethic, she would fuel my desire to be a hard worker.

The fact is, what a mother thinks about the men in her life subtly affects what her son thinks a man should be. If a mother has been hurt by men and holds resentment in her heart, her son is likely to feel guilt and shame about his masculinity. In an effort to compensate, he will probably treat others in controlling, angry, or manipulative ways. For her son's sake, a mom must forgive the people who've hurt her and work to develop a positive attitude toward men.

> What a mother thinks about the men in her life subtly affects what her son thinks a man should be.

This is critical. Much of my ministry involves teaching about fathers and their importance in the development of healthy children. Unfortunately, sometimes the father role gets so overemphasized that mothers feel helpless and incapable of raising masculine boys without the help of a strong father figure. This notion is an oversimplification; many single mothers have raised stellar young men who are very masculine. How? Dr. William Pollack explains in his book, *Real Boys,* "The real issue for the son of a single mother—or the son of any mother, for that matter—is not the presence or absence of a man in the house but the mother's attitude toward men in general."[1]

What Constitutes Real Manhood?

In order for a mother to raise a boy to be a strong, healthy man, she must first have a healthy vision of what constitutes real manhood. Yes, boys will be boys. But one day boys will be men. The world needs moms who have the wisdom, strength, and willingness to birth strong, healthy character traits in their sons. What are some of those traits? Here are four that I think are most important.

The Strength of a Leader

Little boys look forward to growing up and becoming big and strong. When I want to compliment a little girl, I comment on how pretty she looks or how nice her dress is. When I want to compliment a little boy, I comment on how big he is getting or on how strong he is.

I believe manhood is synonymous with strength. God gives a man wide shoulders for a reason. They represent the ability and responsibility to carry others—to shoulder the needs of marriage, family, and community. Every man knows intuitively that he is responsible for the relationships around him, and every boy looks forward to one day becoming that strong man that others can lean

49

on and follow. He looks forward to being a leader. Some people mistakenly think that leaders ride on top of those they lead. They think that others are there to carry them. But Jesus said, "Whoever desires to become great among you shall be your servant" (Mark 10:43).

Real strength and leadership come from the heart. The men who influence and impact other people are the ones who live passionate, dedicated, and sacrificial lives. Because they love hard, they lead well. It is important to have physical strength, but men who change the world do so through heart strength—through love that never quits. A true hero and leader has the heart of a champion. Little boys dream of having such a heart!

A wise mom sees and builds the heart of a leader in her son. Through eyes of love, she sees him one day influencing his marriage, his family, and his community with his heart of gold. She envisions him as a world-changer. That makes her a world-changer too.

Two principles are important here. First, the best motivation is always success. And second, the things that we look for in our children are usually what we see. Stay focused on the leader's heart in your son. Every time he displays leadership character, take advantage of the moment and help him dream of his future. For instance, if he does something nice for a sibling, stop and congratulate him, drawing his attention to the result. You might comment, "I want to congratulate you on what you did. Did you notice the result? When you do something nice for someone because you love them, they look up to you and want to follow your example. That's what leaders do. One day you're going to be a great leader."

But what about the times when he is unleaderlike? How can you change your son's negative behavior? By taking his eyes off of the negative he just did and lifting up a positive vision of what he one day will be doing. The best defense is a good offense! For instance, let's say you catch your son doing something unkind to his sibling. Instead of majoring on the negative he just did, help him dream of the great things he will eventually do. You might say, "I want to remind you of the great leader you are growing up to become. Great leaders don't treat others negatively. If they did, no one would follow them. One day you are going to be a great leader."

When your son does something out of the positive motive of wanting to serve others, you can praise him and talk about the great things he will do one day with a heart like his. When he does something out of a wrong motive, you can, in a positive way, point out how that action does not suit him. A mom who wants to help her son develop the heart of a leader will take every opportunity to confirm that he has a great heart, and he is growing up to be a great man. She will look for ways to draw a picture of the man she is believing him to become.

The Vision of a Provider

As we've said, men are called to provide for those around them. Provision can be defined as "pro-vision"—vision that is positive on behalf of those we are providing for. Our vision is our picture of the future. It starts with a dream and becomes tangible as we apply wisdom, knowledge, motivation, and effort.

Our dreams in life are our deepest expression of what we want—our declaration of our desired future. They are an ideal involving possibilities rather than probabilities, potentials rather than limits. Dreams are not restricted by what we think can or cannot be done or by what our rational mind tells us is or isn't possible. They represent something that we really want as opposed to something we think we can get.

CHAPTER 4: BOYS WILL BE MEN

The ability to see into the future and desire good things for those in our world is a strength greater than physical or financial power. Why? Because physical and financial power both begin with a dream.

Thankfully, boys are born dreamers. Dreaming is how they exercise and prepare to become men who provide.

> The ability to see into the future and desire good things for those in our world is a strength greater than physical or financial power.

A boy may have many talents, skills, and abilities; but without a dream, he will lack the motivation to operate them as he moves into adulthood.

I remember being a daydreamer as a boy. My attention span, according to some, was not long enough. I was continually in trouble for daydreaming in school. But my dreams were not bad dreams; they were always about some great adventure in which I would do something heroic for those around me. We shouldn't discourage that kind of dreaming—maybe just encourage the right timing for it!

A mom is in a great position to encourage her son's ability to dream and see great things for his future. If you catch your son daydreaming, help him develop his "pro-vision" by getting him to talk about his dream. If he's like most boys, it probably involves some adventurous, heroic story, which you can then use to encourage the man you see in your son. "God created you to do great things, just like in your dream," you might say. "You're going to be a great provider."

The Fight of a Protector

In addition to being providers, men have been created to be protectors of their marriages, families, and communities. That's why God made males naturally aggressive: They must be able to put the safety of those around them before their own safety. They must be aggressive enough to overcome their own fear! A normal part of a boy's development is learning to defy fear. In fact, for a boy, growing up is synonymous with overcoming fear. The last thing a boy wants to be known as is a wimp—someone who backs down from challenges because he is afraid.

It's important to note, however, that the battle against fear is a *spiritual* battle. Second Timothy 1:7 says, "For God has not given us a spirit of fear, but of power and of love and of a sound mind." This verse clearly states that fear is a spirit, and it is not from God; therefore, it must be from the devil. John 10:10 tells us that the devil's purpose is "to steal, and to kill, and to destroy." Fear is one

54

of the ways he carries out this purpose in our lives, our families, and our communities.

For twenty-five years of my life, the spirit of fear robbed me. I was controlled by the fear of stuttering. Everything I did revolved around the drive to avoid stuttering in front of people and the painful rejection that might result. I can attest firsthand to the destructive purpose and manipulative power of fear. When God set me free from the fear of stuttering, I declared war! I hated that lying spirit. Whenever it would raise its ugly head in my life, I would charge in defiance and do exactly what the voice of fear said I couldn't do. (You can read more about my testimony and about how to overcome fear in my book, *Limits Were Made to Be Broken*.)

Every boy will have opportunities to be manipulated by fear. Mothers need to help their sons recognize the lying voice of fear and learn to overcome it. Peer pressure is a great teaching opportunity. Peer pressure is just "fear pressure." When you sense your son pulling away from you because of peer pressure—when he hits the age when it's not "cool" to give Mom a kiss, for example—don't give in. Instead, take the blame. Tell his friends, "He's got a fanatical mom. That's why he has to kiss me every day when I drop him off at school." The truth is, a boy really does want affection from his mom; he just reaches a point when he becomes afraid of what his friends will think. And what are they thinking? "I wish my mom were like that!"

When you see your son pushing through fears—jumping out of trees, skateboarding too fast down a hill, or standing up to a bully—encourage the fight of a protector in him by mixing a healthy dose of congratulations with your safety instructions. You might tell him that he's becoming a great man who will never back down to fear. Instead, with wisdom and courage, he will change the world.

Of course, since fear is a spiritual battle, the greatest protection we have is spiritual. God has given men the responsibility of putting on the whole armor of God, so they can stand against the devil's schemes on behalf of their marriages, their families, and their communities (see Ephesians 6:10–18). When you're congratulating your son for his courage, go a step further and tell him about the great spiritual man he's becoming—a true man of God who knows how to fight in the realm of the spirit.

> Since fear is a spiritual battle, the greatest protection we have is spiritual.

The Heart of a Friend

Many men today are lonely. That's tragic, because Steve Biddulph, in his book *Manhood,* states that loneliness is one of the biggest enemies of true manhood.[2] The answer isn't sex. It's friendship. Most men simply don't have a healthy sphere of friends.

No man can accomplish his purpose in life alone, however. Only through relationships can he discover his real purpose and destiny in life. And what is the foundation of all relationships? Friendship. (I believe that Eve became a friend to Adam before she became a wife.) A real man has a heart that nourishes healthy friendships.

Much of the pain in our world today is due to the male need for friendship-building skill. Proverbs 18:24 says, "A man who has friends must himself be friendly." Some people mistakenly think that you get lucky, and friends just happen to you. Not true. According to the wisdom of Solomon, friendships don't come along by luck; they're developed through the exercise of a skill called friendliness. Friends don't happen to you as much as you happen to them.

A boy needs to learn the skill of friendship in order to enjoy a full, satisfying life. As a mom, you can feed and water this skill in your son. When it comes to relationships, you are his best coach.

One great tool at your disposal is the mother-son date. This planned, special time of communication is an ideal opportunity for you to train your son in the art of friendship. On a date, it is best to leave the familiar environment of home, where family members have learned to behave according to specific roles. At home, for example, you may be perceived by your son as the boss, the instructor, the server, or even the opposition. On a date, however, you can simply be a friend.

I recommend having a special date night with your son once a month. If you have two or more sons, plan to meet with each one individually. Going out to a restaurant for a meal is ideal. All boys like to eat, and the time it takes to drive to the restaurant, wait to be served, finish the meal, then drive back home is great relationship-building time. The "law of association" says that you attribute the good feelings of what you are doing to your relationship with the person you are doing it with. The pleasure of enjoying a meal together adds to the good feelings of your developing mother-son friendship.

A date is also an ideal opportunity for you to train your son in good manners—a lost art in our society today. The place where good manners are most noticeable is while eating in public. At a restaurant, you can train your son in proper etiquette. You can teach him how to treat a lady by coaching him to open the door for you; to seat you first; to wait for you to begin eating before he starts eating; and so on. It's sad how few young men have any sense of chivalry or manners. But knowledge builds confidence. Somewhere down the line, your son will thank you for the confidence you helped instill in him about relating to women—and so will your daughter-in-law!

Of course, you can't be your son's only friend. A boy needs friends other than Mom, and a wise mom will encourage her son to develop strong, healthy friendships. The importance of having the right friends cannot be overestimated; after all, friends are among the most powerful influences in our lives.

How can you help your son? By playing an active role in his friendships. Encourage your son to invite his friends over. Feed them. Listen to their dreams. Be a positive factor in their lives.

In the process, take every opportunity to notice and praise the heart of a friend in your son. Since males are more attuned to *doing* than *feeling*, it's up to you to point out how your son's friendships are linked to accomplishing great things. Boys and young men are motivated by the dreams of great future accomplishments. Help your son see how his friendship skills will help him reach great heights as a leader, a provider, and a protector.

If your son doesn't seem to be using healthy friendship skills, look past the present and see the heart of a friend in the man your son is becoming. Find an opportunity to help him dream of his future—a future in which he is displaying the very skills that seem to be lacking. For instance, let's say you hear him speaking negatively about one of his friends. Instead of focusing on what he shouldn't do, help him to see what he really wants to do, which is to be a champion and a winner. When the time is right, talk to him about the champion you see him becoming—the champion who is fiercely loyal and trustworthy, who would never say a negative word about anyone, especially his friends.

> Your son's spiritual, emotional, and physical health is vitally linked to his relationships.

Your son's spiritual, emotional, and physical health is vitally linked to his relationships. To have a healthy, fulfilled life, he will need to develop a heart that is tender, loyal, committed, and not afraid to sacrifice. That's where you come in. As his mom, you have the opportunity to develop a unique relationship with your son. More than anyone else in his life, you have the ability to help him become a real man—one who is a leader, a provider, a protector, and a true friend.

chapter 5

Boys Will Be Dads

We need great dads in our world today. As I travel around the globe, the greatest concern I have is for the scarcity of healthy, functional fathers. A few years ago I wrote a book entitled *The Miracle in a Daddy's Hug*. It is having an impact on dads and their children. The purpose of the book is to help dads see how important they are to their kids and give them the tools they need to be great dads. Fathers desperately need to recognize that every child is a miracle in seed form. They need to understand the tremendous power of their words, time, touch, love, and faith in bringing those miracles to fruition.

The message in *The Miracle in a Daddy's Hug* came as a result of my struggle to help my daughter Danica overcome an eating disorder. She was in an all-out war, and it looked as if she was losing. I had frantically tried everything I could think of to help her, and I was at the end of myself. That's a good place to be, because that is where God takes over! In desperation I cried out to God. Supernaturally, he took all my fear away and gave me an unshakable confidence that everything was going to be all right.

All I needed to do was get this new peace and confidence that was inside me into Danica. That is when I discovered the miracle in a daddy's hug. As I wrapped my arms all the way around my daughter and held her close to my heart, something supernatural transpired. The tears that dripped off my cheek onto her soft brown hair baptized her in Daddy's love. Out of the overflow of my heart, I told her, "Danica, I just plain love you. Nothing you could ever do could make me love you more." (It's so sad when children feel they have to do something to earn Dad's love.) "Nothing you could ever do could make me love you less. You're my princess, and you will always be my princess." This special moment was a turning point in Danica's battle. Today she is a healthy, vital, loving young woman with a healthy family of her own.

Every child looks to Dad for protection, strength, confidence, stability, and identity. Dads really are miracle-producing when it comes to the influence they have on their children. Yet in our world today there is a multitude of children, young and old, reeling in pain over their unmet need for such a daddy. Wherever I teach on the need for functionally healthy fathers, I am shocked at the pain this message evokes. We have a world full of hurting people with voids in their hearts—voids that should have been filled by the influence of a loving, tender, strong, encouraging, functional dad.

The Importance of a Healthy Mom

How can we start to correct this global and generational catastrophe? We can start right here, right now, with moms and sons.

A number of years ago, Helen and I were invited to minister at Mercy Ministries in Nashville, Tennessee. Nancy Alcorn founded Mercy Ministries over twenty years ago to help girls who were in crisis due to eating disorders, unwed pregnancies, drug addictions, sexual abuse, and much more. Our initial meeting with the girls simply involved listening to their stories. The great pain each one related, almost without exception, could be traced back to what Nancy called the daddy vacuum.

I'll never forget Jane's horrific story. (I've changed her name to protect her identity.) She was seventeen, and her dad had sexually abused her since the age of three. At fifteen, he impregnated her. When he found out, he was so furious that he beat her almost to death, then took a coat hanger and performed the abortion. Jane could not even look at me. She wanted nothing to do with fathers. Who could blame her?

During the course of the week, I taught on fathers and daughters, and we saw many great breakthroughs in the hearts of these wounded girls. On my last day, we ended with a question-and-answer session. Near the end, Jane put her hand up. A hush came over the group. She still couldn't look up at me, so I got down on one knee, took her by the hand, and looked up into her eyes.

"What's your question, Jane?" I asked.

Everyone strained to hear. Finally, with great difficulty, she blurted out, "Where do I start?"

"Right here, right now," I responded. "You have to begin to

trust again. Not all fathers are bad. I'm a good dad, and you have a great Dad in heaven who loves you very much." I talked for several minutes about the step of faith she needed to take in order to leave the pain of the past behind her. Then I thanked her for her question and for her willingness to open her heart.

One year later we were invited to come back to Mercy Ministries again. By this time Jane had graduated from the program, and a whole new batch of wounded girls had replaced the ones we'd seen before. On this trip we were privileged to witness a graduation celebration. When the girls graduate, they invite some of the closest people in their lives to come and celebrate with them. For this particular ceremony, one of the girls had invited Jane.

When Jane saw me, she bounded across the room. I hardly recognized her. She glowed! She gave me a big hug and asked if I remembered her. Of course I did! She told me that she had listened over and over to the CD from our question-and-answer session the year before. She had taken my advice, started trusting others with wisdom—and her life had totally changed.

As I stood listening and rejoicing with Jane, a new girl, Sally, sat just two feet behind us. (Again, I've changed her name to protect her identity.) The two girls' stories were the same. I introduced them and asked Jane if she would talk to Sally. She agreed, and about twenty minutes later, I saw them embracing, with tears rolling down their cheeks. The answer to the horrible experience that Jane went through became the answer for Sally too.

Our world needs great fathers, and moms are the answer. Moms who have a healthy image of fatherhood have the ability not only to raise sons who are the answer to our world's needs, but also to raise sons who are capable of enjoying the most fulfilling life possible. I love being a father! For a male, there is not a more impacting, influencing, world-changing role than that of Dad. But to be good dads, most men need help!

The Significance of a Forgiving Mom

Someone needs to stop the downward spiral of dysfunctional dads raising hurting children who raise underprepared sons who become even more dysfunctional dads who raise even more wounded children. Who can that someone be? Mom. We touched on this in the last chapter. A mom who has had a difficult past needs to forgive and let go so that she can move on and become the answer for her son—and for her son's sons.

Forgiveness is a gift that you give yourself and the generations to follow. Many people are confused about forgiveness. They think, "Why should I forgive that person? He doesn't deserve to be forgiven." But forgiveness is not about the other person. It's not even about what he did. It's about

> When you forgive, you let go of yesterday, and you take control of tomorrow.

you. People think that if they forgive, they will be condoning the behavior and thus perpetuating it. No, if you don't forgive, you drag the faults of yesterday into tomorrow, thereby perpetuating the behavior. You let your yesterday control your tomorrow. When you forgive, you let go of yesterday, and you take control of tomorrow.

Sometimes people try to forgive, but they feel incapable; they still hurt, and they can't shake the memory. But forgiveness is not dependent on feelings or memory. Bad things are supposed to hurt. Pain is simply a message telling your brain that something is wrong, so that you may do something to right the wrong. Think of the founder of Mothers against Drunk Driving (MADD). She has used her pain as motivation to do something to right a serious wrong in society. Yet I'm sure it still hurts every time she remembers the death of her thirteen-year-old daughter, Cari, at the hand of a drunk driver.

Forgiveness doesn't mean forgetting. It means releasing the debt a person owes you for having hurt you. Learn what you can from yesterday, and then let go. Your past doesn't owe you anything. Through forgiveness, you can take your life off of hold—stop hanging on, looking backward, expecting a payback—and fully focus on living today to build a great tomorrow. With God's help you can take the negative experiences of the past and convert them into wisdom for the future. In the ledger of your life, God can help you transfer those negative-experience entries from the liabilities column to the assets column. That is how God takes the things that were meant for evil in your life and turns them around for good (see Genesis 50:20).

The Necessity of a Forward-Looking Mom

Moms are the answer for generations to come. I am amazed at how mothers are so generational in their thinking. Years ago, after my first grandchild was born, a young dad asked me, "What's it like to be a grandfather?" I was dazed. I had never had a father ask me that! And yet I recognized that some women, even before they become mothers, ponder such questions.

If we are going to overcome the functional fatherlessness of this past generation, we need moms who can see and believe for healthy, functional fathers in the future. Who are these future fathers? Our sons! The best way to overcome a negative past is with a positive future. Moms who see great dads in their sons will eventually be blessed with healthy grandchildren.

In chapter 3, I described the enormous challenges facing boys in our society today—the huge gap between their physiological development and emotional maturity; the repression of male emotion and sensuality; the perversion of the male ego; and the increasing flood of sexually stimulating media. What is the answer? What can we do to protect and equip our young men?

The answer is communication. Dads need to talk to their sons. They need to talk about sex in a positive way. I don't mean giving a biology report. Boys don't need to hear about the sperm swimming up the fallopian tubes. They need to hear about the upcoming changes in their bodies and how to deal with their physical feelings. Dads need to tell their sons what they wished *their* dads had told them at that age.

Steve Biddulph writes, "With no deep training in masculinity, boys' bodies still turn into men's bodies, but they are not given the inner knowledge and skills to match. It seems obvious that if you

71

live in a man's body, you need to learn how to drive one—preferably from someone who knows how to drive their own."[1]

One of the best ways for dads to communicate on these matters is to share with their sons how they learned to deal with the changes and feelings in their own bodies. This will prepare their sons educationally while at the same time promoting a sense of father-son intimacy and friendship. The problem is that in the last generation, dads didn't talk to their sons, and now much of this generation doesn't know how to talk to its sons. We need to break the cycle. We need to raise a generation of adult men who can talk to their sons and model the emotional sensitivity of healthy manhood. This, again, is where moms are the answer.

> The mess we have in our society did not happen overnight, and it won't go away overnight.

The mess we have in our society did not happen overnight, and it won't go away overnight. It was generations in the making, and it might be generations in the fixing. God's plan is for a boy to learn the tools of communication from his mother, and watch his father model them in his marriage. He needs to learn about real manhood from Mom, and then see Dad model emotional sensitivity, affection,

72

and a godly male ego in his home. He needs Mom to encourage him in his masculinity, and then see Dad be a leader, a provider, a protector, and a friend. His understanding of sex needs to be healthy and positive, based on fatherly instruction, friendship, and coaching. With this equipping, a boy is prepared to become a real man and build a healthy marriage and family. This is the positive cycle where male and female complement and complete each other, and God says, "Very good!"

As a mom, you can make this generational difference. By training your son to understand, respect, honor, and communicate with a woman, you can help begin a new cycle of healing. By encouraging him to become the man you know he can be, you can give him the tools he needs to develop healthy friendships, find a wife who complements him, and build a healthy marriage. Then he can begin a new cycle as a healthy husband and a healthy father, modeling the positive strengths of real manhood to the next generation—and multiplying them to the generations to come.

A Letter to My Mom

Dear Mom,

Your life is an incredible model of strength, persistence, consistency, and selflessness. Your example is a constant goal before me that encourages and empowers me to climb higher, dream bigger, and live louder. Whenever I wrestle with thoughts like I can't, *or* It's too hard, *I just think of you, and the battle is over. You really are Superwoman!*

I can remember the multitude of times I yelled, "Mom, watch me!" as I jumped off the couch wearing a cape on my back, performed my first summersaults, or took off down the street on my first bike ride. You were my best cheerleader. When I decided at eight years old that I would be an artist, you celebrated my aspiration and hung up my paintings like trophies. And then I decided to be a musician.... The hours you labored, listening to me practice and then pretending to enjoy my every song—you helped me soar.

Every boy needs a mom who will champion him, and I certainly was championed by a champion. Any mom who can raise eleven wonderful, healthy, happy children is a CHAMPION in my book. I want to thank you for the abundance of parenting lessons you taught us all. I'm sure you were not aware that you were teaching, and we certainly were not aware that we were learning. Who would have guessed that a few decades down the road, your little Johnny would be a dad, a granddad, and a pastor writing books on parenting? Thanks for being my teacher!

And Mom, thanks for never giving up. I apologize for the myriad of troubles I caused that would have sent most mothers over the edge—but not you. Your persistence and unwavering commitment to family has forged the foundation that I aspire to build on and pass on to the generations to come.

You truly are the virtuous woman that Proverbs 31:28–31 talks about:

Her children rise up and call her blessed;

Her husband also, and he praises her:

"Many daughters have done well,

But you excel them all."

Charm is deceitful and beauty is passing,

    But a woman who fears the LORD, she shall
        be praised.

Give her of the fruit of her hands,

And let her own works praise her in the gates.

Mom, Helen and I, along with our children and grandchildren and all the generations to come, salute you. You are my hero! I love you.

John

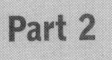

Part 2

What *Dads* Need to Know about *Daughters*

From God, a man can learn the qualities and characteristics that will make him the kind of dad his daugher needs him to be—and the kind of dad God always intended him to be

—Helen Burns

chapter
6

It's a Girl!

It's a girl!" Those three little words create a rush of joy and anticipation for every new dad—typically followed by a healthy dose of fear and apprehension. How do you raise this darling little princess wrapped in pink blankets from healthy infancy to healthy adulthood? How do you teach her to navigate her personal journey of life through a big and sometimes dangerous world?

I know that's what my father was thinking on the day I was born. Every year on my birthday he would tell me the story of the day of my birth (which happened over fifty years ago). My parents were new immigrants in Canada, and money was hard to come by; so my father had to finish his day's work at the steel factory before taking the bus to the hospital to see his wife and his new baby girl. In his excitement, when he reached the hospital, he stepped off the bus and ran smack into the sharp corner of the wooden post of the bus stop, opening a big gash in his head and almost knocking himself out. Rather than going to the emergency ward to get stitched up, however, he came straight to the nursery. He took his first look at me—his second daughter born in just eighteen months—and soon found himself overwhelmed by what lay ahead. He was already in a new country with a new culture and a new language. Now he was also in a new family filled with only females. Talk about a challenge!

Many years later my husband, John, also discovered the joy of raising a house full of daughters. All three of our girls were born in a short space of three and a half years. I have been amazed and often amused as I've watched this very masculine man rise to the challenge of raising daughters from infancy through the teen years and on to adulthood. It is from this wonderful perch of being a woman raising a household of women, watching the husband I love learn, develop, and grow as a dad and granddad, that I share with you now. There are certain things every dad needs to know about raising a daughter. We'll talk about some of those things in the pages that follow.

Before we get started, though, I want to make one thing clear. We live in an imperfect world. That means there is no such thing as a perfect father this side of heaven. But the other side of heaven—well, that's a different story. Our heavenly Father *is* perfect. From God, a man can learn the qualities and characteristics that will make him the kind of dad his daughter needs him to be—and the kind of dad God always intended him to be. It is very easy for a man to become a father. But it takes a very special, loving, committed man to be a good daddy to his daughter.

> There is no such thing as a perfect father this side of heaven.

Since you're reading this book, I'm assuming that you're one of those special men—or at least, you aspire to be. Congratulations! I salute you. No one can take your place in your daughter's life. Yes, your daughter needs her mom; but she also needs *you*. Turn the page, and we'll talk about why.

chapter 7

The Challenge

Have you ever noticed that when a grown man speaks to a little boy, he uses a big, booming voice; but when he speaks to a little girl, he uses a gentle, high-pitched whisper? Why does this happen? Because from early on, a little girl's "differentness" is evident—a fact that becomes more and more apparent as she grows and matures through the many stages of her life.

The fact is, God created girls different on purpose—a heaven-designed purpose. He formed Eve out of the material that he removed from Adam. Consequently, Adam was left missing

83

something in order to *be* complete; Eve was left searching for where she belonged in order *to* complete. A female's desire is to complete a male. And who is the male in a little girl's life? Her daddy.

Every little girl wants to be the princess who wins her daddy's heart. Dad is her very first Prince Charming. She longs to know that she's adored, accepted by, and approved of by Daddy.

> Every little girl wants to be the princess who wins her daddy's heart.

She wants to be noticed by him, to be seen—not just for her accomplishments, but for who she is. As she grows up, her self-concept as a female and her self-worth as a young woman is shaped primarily through the relationship she has with her dad. She sees and comes to recognize her value through the reflection in his eyes.

That's how it was for me. I am so blessed to have always felt the love, warmth, and acceptance of my father. When I was growing up, I was aware that Dad's eyes would light up and a big smile would cross his face whenever I walked into the room. I felt the wonder that every girl longs for—the wonder of being loved unconditionally by Daddy.

That's how it has been for my three daughters too. Angela,

Danica, and Ashley have always cherished their dad's acceptance and approval. When they were little, I would take them shopping for special occasion dresses (at Easter or Christmas, for example), and they would always choose dresses that they thought John would like—dresses that eventually came to be called "daddy dresses." The girls loved being noticed by Daddy! Getting dressed up was for the purpose of delighting him. John was always generous with his *oohs* and *aahs,* which would make them giggle to no end—and bring joy to my heart.

His love for all three girls has been generous and unconditional. All their lives he has told them, "I will love you always, and I will love you forever. Nothing you could ever do could make me love you more. Nothing you could ever do could make me love you less. You will always be my princess."

Where has John found the strength and confidence to love his daughters so completely? I can point to one source: his relationship with his heavenly Father. Thankfully, God does not accept any of us based on our performance, our looks, the size of our bank account, our job, or anything else that this world values so highly. God loves us simply because we are his children. "How great is the love the Father has lavished on us, that we should be called children of God!" (1 John 3:1 NIV). To *lavish* is to give freely, extravagantly, profusely, and abundantly. Through his Son, Jesus, God opened the door for each of us to be loved lavishly and unconditionally by a perfect Father. A father who knows the love of his heavenly Father can, in turn, lavish the love he has received from God on his own children.

Intuitively, little girls know that they were created to love and be loved by Daddy. But the sad truth is that many women grow up with dads who, for one reason or another, never know the love of their heavenly Father—or an earthly father, for that matter. As a result, these girls are often raised by dads who are distant, angry, abusive, or simply absent. Their definition of *father* becomes synonymous with disapproval, disappointment, or rejection. When this is a daughter's experience, she may have a hard time connecting with God the Father (even though God is a perfect Father who loves her with unconditional, everlasting love). Sensing an empty place in her life, she may try to fill the vacuum with accomplishments and achievements, believing that somehow these things will make up for her perceived deficits—and maybe, just maybe, gain the acceptance and approval she longs to receive from Dad.

CHAPTER 7: THE CHALLENGE
The Daddy Vacuum

If only every dad would understand how important he is to his little girl! A father has a huge influence on his daughter's life—for good or for bad. Whether he's aware of it or not, he plays a significant, irreplaceable role in shaping his daughter's world.

I have had the privilege of traveling and ministering around the world, and I have noticed a malady among women that seems to be universal. To describe it, John and I use the term the "daddy vacuum." You see, in the heart of every little girl, there is a big, open space that is reserved for Daddy. When a father doesn't fill that space—when he's abusive, emotionally unavailable, or physically absent—a girl grows up with a daddy emptiness. The emptiness that she feels creates a vast amount of pain, as well as numerous roadblocks to future healthy relationships with men. Sadly, large numbers of women around the globe are heartsick and unable to develop positive male-female relationships, because they've never experienced the gentle, caring, unconditional love of a dad. This is a loss, and the results are catastrophic—not only for these women, but for society as a whole.

Numerous studies have shown that girls reach puberty younger, become sexually active earlier, and are more likely to get pregnant in their teen years if their fathers are absent from their homes and lives.[1] I think this is very predictable in light of the great need every female has for affection. These young women are not "bad"; they just have a desperate longing for the closeness, bonding, love, and security they never received as little girls from active, devoted, and caring fathers. God created them with that longing. And he created dads to fulfill it.

> Only as we rebuild this biblical foundation for healthy families can we produce healthy communities.

Unfortunately, many children are growing up today without the benefit of a father in the home. Perhaps more than any other factor, this pervasive fatherlessness is shaping our culture. The large number of fathers who have abdicated their commitment to their families has created a huge, gaping crevice in society at large. One result is that many women have begun to believe they don't need men—that men are nothing but trouble, and they can do just fine without them. Nothing could be further from the truth! Women *and* men desperately need to go back to the foundation of all truth—the Word of God—which clearly shows us God's intention for male-female relationships. According to God's plan, the foundation of a healthy family is a healthy husband-wife relationship, developed through intimate communication and mutual respect and understanding between a man and a woman. Only as we rebuild this biblical foundation for healthy families can we produce healthy communities, which in turn can lead to a healthier society for all.

Impossible Standards

Since you are reading this book, I believe you must be a dad who has chosen to *be there* for your daughter. There will be no daddy vacuum for your little girl—not if you have anything to say about it!

But let me warn you: the task ahead of you isn't easy. We live in a very conditional world, where love, appreciation, and acceptance are based on factors such as looks, money, achievement, and success. "I'll accept you if you do this, this, and this," the world says. One of the key challenges dads face is how to love their daughters unconditionally, regardless of how those daughters measure up to the world's conditions.

A significant part of the challenge has to do with the natural tendency of men to be competitive, which sometimes leads them to pressure their children to be "the best." While it is a wonderful thing for a dad to want the very best for his daughter, it's vital that fathers understand that what this world deems "best" and what really *is* best are usually two different things. The world's definition of "best" is based on faulty standards that no daughter can live up to—or should, if she is going to grow up to be a healthy woman with healthy relationships.

What are those standards? Here are three of the most common ones.

1. A Standard of Beauty. The world has set such an impossible standard for beauty that many attractive young women are literally killing themselves trying to achieve it. The rise in the occurrence of eating disorders, depression, and suicide among teenage girls and young women is truly scary. For many girls, self-esteem is at an all-time low.

What's the problem? One glance at the magazine rack in the grocery store checkout line gives us the answer. The covers of teen and women's magazines are overflowing with digitally enhanced photographs of women who conform to an impossibly perfect ideal. I remember watching an interview with Cindy Crawford, a stunning supermodel, who told the audience that even *she* didn't look like Cindy Crawford until she spent two hours in hair and makeup. She went on to say that despite having the best photographers in the world and spending so much time preparing for a photo shoot, the photo editors still had to use the wonders of digital technology to make her thighs thinner, her legs longer, her breasts larger, her hair thicker, and her lips fuller. What we see on the magazine cover is not real, she said; it is an illusion that no one can live up to—nor should they try to!

Sadly, many dads don't help their daughters in this area. They never tell their girls, "You're so beautiful to me." Or if they do, they contradict their message by the inappropriate reactions and comments they make about other women. Sometimes girls who feel rejected by Daddy for one reason or another end up assuming that their lack of physical perfection is at fault. Plastic surgeons are getting rich from their endless pursuits of a false and dangerous standard.

2. A Standard of Scholastic Achievement. It is probably natural for a father to want to have a daughter who has both beauty *and* brains. Hopefully, he knows enough to look at his little girl through the eyes of love and deem her positively gorgeous. As for brains, a good dad *should* encourage his daughter to do well in school and work at her optimum level. After all, that's what's best for *her*. When it comes to scholastic success, however, there's a big difference between encouragement and pressure. Encouragement comes from love and from having the other person's best interests at heart; pressure comes from selfishness (there's that competitive nature again) and from having your own interests at heart.

Unfortunately, many a daughter, based on her dad's words and reactions, comes to the conclusion, "Daddy will love me and notice me more if I am smarter than the next person." No little girl should ever feel compelled to gain her father's approval through her scholastic accomplishments. Why should she have to work for something that should be freely given?

3. A Standard of Talent. How many dads spend countless hours at their kids' soccer practices, baseball games, and gymnastics meets? I think such devotion is fantastic, as long as the goal is to help the children do what they want to do and what is good for them. For a daughter especially, the relationship that develops with Dad driving to and from practices and games is as valuable as the games themselves—maybe more so.

Unfortunately, we have all heard about the way competitive sports have been getting out of hand in recent years. The competition is no longer between the kids on the field; it's between the parents on the sidelines! Dads are being thrown out of ice rinks and off soccer fields because they are behaving so badly. Apparently, too many dads (and some moms) are deriving their sense of value from how well their children do in sports or other endeavors. These adults need to be the ones teaching their kids: winning at all costs is not winning!

Yes, it's good for a dad to encourage his daughter to use her talents and develop her skills to the best of her ability. But many parents have a tendency to only notice what is lacking in their children's performances and point out those deficiencies. A dad, with his natural sense of competitiveness, can be especially critical of a daughter's performance in competition. In a little girl's mind, this criticism often translates into a sense of inadequacy and an unhealthy pressure to become "what Daddy wants," rather than the unique and special woman God intends her to be.

Through Daddy's Eyes

A dad's job is to look at his daughter and, through eyes of unconditional love and unwavering faith, see a beautiful, confident, amazing young woman in the making. A dad should never try to squeeze his little girl into a preferred mold but rather encourage her to be molded by God—according to heaven's standards, not the world's. What happens to a little girl who grows up knowing that she is loved unconditionally by Daddy, who knows that the most important man in her life does not judge her by the world's standards but sees her through the eyes of unconditional acceptance and love? She eventually becomes a whole and healthy woman, wife, and mom, capable of relating, loving, growing, and nurturing a family of her own—and influencing generations to come.

chapter

8

Dads Are
the Answer

Daddy's home!" When my daughters were young, that announcement would send them running to the garage to greet Mr. Wonderful, who would sweep them up in his arms and lavish them generously with hugs, kisses, and tickles. The girls were blessed, but so was John. What father wouldn't want to be celebrated upon his entrance into his very own castle?

Every little girl needs Dad to "be home" for her. She needs him to be available physically and emotionally. Not twenty-four hours a day, of course; a dad needs to work and provide for his family. That's a critical part of his role as a father. But whether he realizes it or not, his presence has the ability to produce a sense of calm and safety in his daughter's life—a wonderful feeling of "Daddy's here, so all is well with the world."

How I've treasured the moments in my life when I've sensed the closeness and security of my own father's presence! Just that simple phrase, "Daddy's home," brings back memories of my childhood—simple, small moments when I felt safe and cared for by Dad. I remember . . .

. . . my tiny hand held firmly in his strong grip as we crossed a busy street. The cars were flying by, but I felt no imminent danger, because Daddy was holding my hand.

. . . sitting on my bed with my sister, both of us dressed in our pajamas and cuddled up on either side of Dad, listening to him tell us silly bedtime stories that he made up as he went along. I still remember a few of those stories, because Dad made me the heroine. I liked that!

. . . lying in bed and hearing the distinct sound of our old, rickety Volkswagen Beetle driving up the street, as Dad made his way home after his shift at the factory. I knew that in a moment, the lights of his car would be reflecting on my bedroom wall; and a few moments after that, he would be in the bedroom, tucking my sister and me under the covers and kissing us good night.

My dad was always there for me. Looking back, I am eternally grateful. I am very aware that his steady, reliable, loving presence played a significant role in shaping me into the woman and mother I am today.

A Dad Teaches His Daughter How to View Herself

You see, a little girl grows up in a world of relationships. Over time, her sense of self-worth and value is defined primarily by her relationships with others; it's how she discovers purpose and meaning in life. Her feelings of safety and security, too, are packaged in the arms of her relationships—especially her relationship with Dad.

In the last chapter, we said that the world sets false, unrealistic standards of beauty, scholastic achievement, and talent that are impossible for a young girl to live up to. And she shouldn't have to! Trying to live up to such standards is hazardous to a girl's mental, emotional, physical, and spiritual health. What's the answer? Dad. As a father, you play a key role in discrediting these standards and

97

encouraging your little princess to be who she is, not who the world wants her to be.

True Beauty

For example, to keep your daughter from falling under the influence of the world's standard of beauty, make sure she knows that

> Make sure she knows that in your eyes she is absolutely stunning. Tell her often how amazing and truly beautiful she is.

in your eyes, she is absolutely stunning. Tell her often how amazing and truly beautiful she is. By doing so, you will encourage her to love herself and to respect and value her body. Any comments that you make about her body or appearance must be positive. If you make negative comments, she may begin to think, *If Dad can't accept me the way I am, what man ever will?* Right now you are the loudest male voice speaking into her life. Make it an affirmative and encouraging voice!

Of course, having an approving father is not a fail-safe guarantee that your daughter will never deal with body-image issues. As John tells in his book, *The Miracle in a Daddy's Hug*, our daughter, Danica, struggled with an eating disorder as a teenager. But through God's help and John's steady, unconditional love, Danica was able to grow into the beautiful, healthy woman, wife, and mother she is today. I can tell you from experience: your love and positive encouragement as a dad will go a long way toward carrying your daughter through any challenges she may face in this or any other area of her life.

So will your positive treatment of other women in her presence. The fact is, most of what we teach our children is caught, not taught. Females are perceptive; your daughter will notice how you treat other women and how you speak about them and their bodies. Some men think little about making lewd or disrespectful comments about the women they see on the street, on TV, or in the movies—even when their own daughters are present. It's important to recognize that you are the gateway to your daughter's understanding about how men view women in relation to their bodies and their sexuality. For your little girl's sake, be sure that you speak, act, and carry yourself in a respectful and wholesome manner around other women.

Making the Grade

To keep your daughter from measuring herself according to the world's standard of scholastic achievement, go ahead and encourage her to do her best in school. Celebrate her accomplishments, whether she gets straight A's or works hard to finally bring that C up to a B. At the same time, make sure she knows that your love for her and your approval of her is unconditional. A girl who is secure in her dad's approval tends to do far better scholastically, feel better about her future, approach her career choices with more confidence, and be more successful at whatever she chooses than a girl who senses disapproval from Dad.

The key is encouragement, not pressure. A daughter who feels a lot of pressure from Dad to "be the best" in school or other academic endeavors may become so resentful and discouraged that

The key is encouragement, not pressure.

she stops trying her best. If you really want to help your daughter succeed in the future, you need to partner with her, encourage her, and be that calm, steady voice that speaks words of hope and strength to her. Don't compare her to others or pressure her to be *the* best; encourage her to be *her* best. Help her to appreciate the unique person that God created her to be.

After all, these are exciting days for women. Your daughter can grow up to be a CEO, a physicist, a Supreme Court judge, an airline pilot—virtually anything she desires to be. As her dad, your words of encouragement will speak volumes to her heart and breathe life into her dreams.

Spotlight on Talent

To help your daughter avoid comparing herself to others according to the world's standard of talent, find ways to celebrate her uniqueness and look for ways to bring attention to it. When you notice a special talent or gifting in your little girl, tell her. You will be shouting volumes of approval. Always look for the best in your daughter and shine your spotlight of support on those positive areas of her life. Praise her when she does something well, whether it's a small thing or a big deal. A young woman will naturally flourish in a home where she is celebrated for who she is—and where she is given permission to develop into the special person she is becoming.

Actress Reese Witherspoon is a perfect example. When she gave her acceptance speech at the 2006 Academy Awards for her Oscar-winning role in the movie *Walk the Line*, she said, "I am so blessed to have my family here tonight. My mother and father are here. And I just want to say thank you so much for everything, for being so proud of me. It didn't matter if I was making my bed or making a movie. They never hesitated to say how proud they were of me. And that means so very much to a child. So thank you, Mom and Dad."[1]

Isn't it amazing how words of approval stick in our hearts and minds forever? Recently I was talking with a friend about one of my roles in life—being a pastor's wife—and how I ended up doing what I am doing today. I was instantly reminded of a time when my father's words of approval spoke directly to my heart as a little girl. I was not yet in primary school. In those years my father struggled greatly with debilitating asthma, and I found myself loving the role of helping Mom take care of him.

I was probably more of a nuisance than a help, but Dad would always tell me what a great nurse I was and how much I reminded him of his beautiful mother. My grandmother, a pastor's wife, had been renowned in her community for her gracious and loving acts. I never had the opportunity to meet her, because she died before I was a year old and she lived many thousands of miles away. But to this day, I desire to develop the character qualities of this amazing woman who raised my father. I want to be the kind of pastor's wife that she was. When I get to heaven, she is one of the first people I want to meet.

The comparison my father made, coupled with his delight over me despite his severe illness, spoke volumes to my heart as a little girl. It still speaks to me today. How incredible!

A Dad Protects His Daughter

I believe that dads have another key role, in addition to helping their daughters overcome the pressure to measure themselves according to the world's standards. It is the job of fathers to protect their little girls—to the extent that it's possible—from injury and harm in an increasingly dangerous world.

I know my parents were very protective of me when I was growing up. John and I, as parents, were very protective of our three daughters when they were young. Now I am watching my three grown daughters raise their children in the same protective manner. It's funny. As a child I grumbled—and later, my girls grumbled—about having such overprotective parents; and yet we all went on to follow the example that was set for us. Why? Because as girls and young women, we always felt protected and safe. We knew we were being rescued from hidden traps and shielded from any number of deadly hazards, thanks to our parents—and thanks especially to those huge, outstretched, fatherly arms that encompassed us. We were kept perfectly safe in a very unsafe world, and it wasn't coincidental; it was completely intentional.

I remember one night in particular when the blessings of having a protective father really hit home. I was a cheerleader for our high school, and a group of us girls became separated from the rest of the team after an away game. We ended up missing the team bus and fending for ourselves in an unfamiliar part of town.

> Knowing that my dad would always come to my rescue made me feel so safe.

It was late, and some of the girls were afraid—of the neighborhood, yes, but also of what their parents would say or do to them when they got home. I wasn't alarmed, however. I knew I could always call my dad and he would come rescue me and my friends, no matter where we were or what time it was. Although I could expect to get a lecture on what not to do in the future, I could also expect Dad to thank me for doing the right thing by calling him. Which, of course, is exactly what I did!

Knowing that my dad would always come to my rescue made me feel so safe. Ultimately, his firm and loving protection created a desire in me to look for my own man of strength to marry. A man who would be valiant and courageous. A man who would always be there to look out for me and my little brood of "chicks." A man like my dad.

I am all for people learning from their mistakes, but I believe that experience is not the best teacher for our children; guidance and wisdom are much better. As a dad, you can provide this all-important guidance and wisdom for your daughter. The way the world is today, being a protective father is far better than being a permissive father.

Protection, Not Control

It's also better than being a controlling father. Sometimes a dad can go too far and move from a protective role to a controlling role in his daughter's life.

I know everyone has heard a story about a young suitor coming to meet his girlfriend's father, only to find the old man polishing his shotgun. This actually happened to my husband on the day I first introduced him to my father. I was excited to bring my new friend, Johnny, home to meet Dad. But as we walked into the kitchen, there was my dad, cleaning his hunting rifle and barely looking up to say hello. I was mortified! In that one instance, I think it's safe to say, my dad went a little overboard. (In his defense, Dad is an avid hunter, and it was hunting season.)

I don't recommend that you clean your rifle when your daughter wants to introduce you to a potential boyfriend. It may appear that you want to control your daughter's relationships because you don't trust her judgment. That's not a message you want her to receive; it's likely to hurt your relationship in the long run. At the time of my own rifle-and-boyfriend episode, my father and I already had such a trusting relationship that I didn't mistake his protection for control, and my feelings for him weren't swayed. Neither, obviously, were my feelings for Johnny!

There's a huge difference between being a protective dad and being a controlling dad. A protective dad is one who sets clear boundaries for his daughter, with the goal of helping her grow up in a safe and wholesome environment. A controlling father, on the other hand, tries to take over his daughter's life and manipulate her with fear. Let me encourage you, for the sake of your father-daughter relationship: Protect your daughter, but don't try to control her!

Safe at Home

One of the most important ways you can protect your daughter is by creating a safe and healthy home environment. Here are some ways you can do that.

1. Talk to her often about what is and isn't appropriate behavior. When your daughter is comfortable and secure in your presence, she will develop a healthy instinct for what isn't "right." I remember a time when I was twelve or thirteen years old, and I was baby-sitting for neighbors who were friends of our family. While I was there, I was approached in an inappropriate way by the man in that home. His advance made me feel very uncomfortable, and I knew immediately it was wrong. I went straight home and told my parents about the incident. They assured me they would take care of the situation and that I would never have to baby-sit for that family again.

Years later I realized how wonderful it was to have been able to tell my parents anything, without any shame or fear of what they might say or do. I knew they would always believe me and protect me. Not every daughter is so blessed. Many women I have counseled have told me stories about their childhoods in which they accepted abuse, stayed in abusive situations, or hid abuse because they didn't feel safe telling their parents what was going on. Don't put your daughter in that situation. Be the kind of dad she can talk to and count on.

2. Know where she is and who she's with. While there will be many times when your daughter isn't under your direct care—at school, for example—you can still protect her by being aware and confident about wherever she is. Check up on her and make sure she is where she is supposed to be, or where she said she would be. My dad did this with me; John did it with our girls; and I recommend you do it too. In addition to knowing where she is, know who she is with. Get to know her friends, and do everything you can to make your home a great place for them to hang out. Because John and I wanted our daughters and their friends to be around our home a lot, we made sure it was a fun place to be. We kept the atmosphere upbeat with lots of games, videos, music— and, of course, food! Our girls' friends looked forward to coming over. They knew they were always welcome in our home.

3. Do what's safe, not what's popular. Yes, our home was fun. But sometimes John and I made decisions that were unpopular. For example, when our girls were growing up, we didn't allow them to attend sleepover parties at friends' homes. This didn't help us win any popularity contests with our children, their friends, or some-times their friends' parents. But we were more concerned with the girls' safety than our own popularity.

The statistics on the number of women who are sexually

abused at some point in their lifetimes are staggering. About 90 percent of abuse is committed by people who are known to their victims; only 10 percent of abusive incidents involve strangers. And where are some of the most common places that young girls are sexually abused? In the homes of friends or relatives.[2]

Don't get me wrong. John and I didn't live in fear and paranoia about our daughters being abused. But we did feel that the safest route was to find creative alternatives to sleepovers, so the girls wouldn't feel they were missing out on fun and excitement. Yes, our girls were sometimes upset with us when a sleepover was planned and we said no. But John and I felt we could live with a little upset, if it meant the girls were safer as a result. The pain and consequences of even one abusive incident can last a lifetime.

> The pain and consequences of even one abusive incident can last a lifetime.

4. Become Internet-savvy. These days there is a new and potentially dangerous intruder in most of our homes: the Internet. To protect your daughter from Internet predators, pornography, and other hazards on the World Wide Web, learn as much as you can about computers, the Internet, and how they work. Always keep your computer in an open place in your home, where your whole family can see it and use it. Check regularly to see what sites your daughter has been visiting. Keep an eye on the kind of material she is viewing and have discussions about it.

Make sure you teach your daughter to never give out any personal information about herself, her family, or her friends. Sadly, many predators are out there in cyberspace, trying to pry this kind of information from unsuspecting young girls. Be very cautious about chat rooms in particular, and acquaint yourself with basic chat-message language—the informal, shorthand vocabulary that has evolved in the world of instant messaging. That way you can know whether or not your daughter is being safe and wise in her communications over the Internet.

Whatever you do, don't hide your head in the sand and just hope for the best. Computers are here to stay. It's up to you to stay involved and connected in your daughter's world.

5. Be media-aware. As a dad, you really need to know what kind of music your daughter is listening to and what kinds of movies and television shows she is watching. Certainly, there are some good movies being made and some good music being produced. There are a few good TV programs to watch and a few good magazines to read. But there is much, much more that isn't good. Most of today's media messages create negative peer pressure, encouraging our children to embrace the relativistic and immoral value systems of the world. Your job is to keep your eyes and ears open, stay connected, and ask questions. Talk about the issues raised on the TV shows or movies your daughter watches—not in a condemning manner, but with genuine concern and interest. Help her to make wise choices about what she allows to come into her eyes, ears, and mind through the media.

6. Be willing to be the fall guy. Many times our daughters—like all children—felt the enormous pressure of wanting to fit in with the crowd. They wanted to do whatever all the other kids were doing. Being protective parents, however, John and I often said no to activities that other parents allowed. "It's not fair," the girls would cry. "All our friends get to do _____. Why can't we? What will our friends think if we're the only ones who don't show up?"

John always answered, "Just blame me." As their father, he was perfectly willing to be the fall guy. He told the girls, "Just tell your friends that you have a mean old dad who won't let you do anything." He assured them that his shoulders were big enough to handle the full brunt of the criticism and blame. If there was a sleepover or an unsupervised party or dance they weren't allowed to go to, they could simply say, "It's my dad's fault." The girls weren't always happy with our decisions—at least not publicly. But secretly, they were often thankful that Dad gave them an out from potentially sticky or uncomfortable situations.

A Born Hero

I think every dad is born to be a hero in his daughter's life. A hero who protects her from harm and danger. A hero who is willing to sacrifice everything in order to do what's best for his princess. A hero who is more concerned with doing what is right than doing what is easy. A hero who knows what his daughter needs is a father, not just a friend.

I can look back and remember so many times when my father stood up for what was right in my life, no matter how "unfair" I thought he was being; no matter how "ridiculous" his curfew seemed at the time; no matter how much I disagreed with his "off-base" opinion about a potentially unhealthy relationship. Today I know something I didn't know then: those are the things that a hero does. A hero steps between his daughter and danger. He stands strong and firm, knowing that his job is to guide, guard, and protect his special entrustment from God.

Every little girl longs to have a hero in her life—and a loving, caring, protecting father is the best man for the job. For every daughter, Dad is the answer.

Girls Will Be Women

I remember the day I had an illuminating conversation with my brother, Jim, the father of three awesome sons and one sweet daughter. My brother, who races motorcycles, hunts, fishes, and is into every manner of extreme sports—and has raised his three sons to do the same—was brought to his knees in one unsuspecting moment. I must admit it made me chuckle to hear him tell me about the time he was driving in his pickup truck and heard the song "Butterfly Kisses" on the radio. "Butterfly Kisses" is a heart-wrenching ballad by

Bob Carlisle about a daddy's love for his little girl as he watches her grow into a beautiful young woman. Poor Jim. The song completely undid him.

What is it about little girls growing up that sends shivers into the hearts of dads everywhere? I am a mother, so I can only guess; but I believe that God put inside the heart of every father the desire and responsibility to treat his daughter with tender affection.

Isaiah was speaking about our heavenly Father when he wrote, "He tends his flock like a shepherd: He gathers the lambs in his arms and carries them close to his heart" (Isaiah 40:11 NIV). For earthly fathers, this scripture provides a perfect model. It wonderfully depicts the gentleness, tenderness, and security that a daddy's arms can provide as he carries his daughter close to his heart. That fatherly, shepherdlike care is so important for a little girl to know; for as she learns to trust her father's heart, she ultimately learns to trust her own heart.

The Necessity of a Daddy's Affection

One of the greatest needs every woman has is for affection—pure and simple, no strings attached, no sexual overtones, no ulterior motives. By definition, affection is a tender feeling, emotion, or fondness that one person has toward another person. It is an expression of love that symbolizes approval and security. A woman experiences affection when a man holds her with warmth and tenderness, and she knows without a doubt that she is perfectly safe and purely loved.

So where is the healthiest place for a young woman to learn how to receive this kind of pure affection? In her daddy's arms as she is growing up. That's where she learns to be cherished and treasured for who she is, without being regarded as a sexual object in any way. The fact is, the home environment in which a girl is raised is a strong determinant of the kind of affection she will gravitate toward as an adult. I am sure you are familiar with the expression, "looking for love in all the wrong places." Seeking unhealthy affection is very predictable behavior for a young woman who, as a child, lacked an affectionate relationship with her dad.

A number of years ago I went out on a special date with my father. Dad had just heard John teach a seminar on the value of a father "dating" his daughter on a regular basis. Dad was sad that he hadn't developed a dating ritual with me when I was young; but to his credit, he realized it was never too late to start.

What an endearing picture he made as he walked up to my front door to pick me up, obviously a bit uneasy about this new adventure! He took me to a lovely restaurant, and we enjoyed a delicious meal together. Then, as we were getting ready to leave, he asked me a question. He had hesitated to ask it earlier, and he was nervous as he finally put it into words: had I ever felt hurt by the way he had distanced himself from me, in the years when I was going through puberty and becoming a young woman?

I was surprised by his question and assured him that I had always felt loved and treasured by him at every stage of my life. I told him he was my hero, and I couldn't love him more. Still, he felt the need to apologize and ask for my forgiveness. He had never wanted to hurt me, he said; and if he had in any way, he was very sorry for it.

When I got home, I told my husband about this unusual conversation with my dad. It became a marked moment for John, because Dad's question related directly to the feelings he was experiencing in his relationship with our eldest daughter, Angela. Angela was at that no-longer-a-child-but-not-yet-a-woman age— the same age I was when my father started feeling uncomfortable and uncertain about how to show affection toward me. John realized that instead of backing away from Angela, he needed to "double the touch" and press through any barriers that might keep him from showing affection to his daughter. Since then, both John and I—not to mention our girls—have been so grateful to my dad for having had the courage to ask his question. John was deeply impacted by it; and as a result, it became a powerful protection for our girls in all their future relationships with men.

You see, as a girl begins to enter puberty, she often suddenly become modest and very aware of her changing body. Often a father's reaction is to think that she doesn't want or need his affection anymore—that somehow it's no longer appropriate. Nothing could be further from the truth.

A dad who is comfortable with showing affection through all the stages of his daughter's life sets up a safety barrier against mistreatment and abuse in all her future relationships. When a blossoming young woman experiences affection within the safe and healthy boundaries of a father-daughter relationship, she learns to set healthy boundaries with others. In my own case, because I was loved, cherished, and protected by Dad—the most significant man in my life besides John—I grew up feeling comfortable with myself, and I expected to be treated well in other relationships.

119

Ultimately, Dad's love showed me what I needed to look for in the man who would one day become my husband and the father of my children.

As a father, you don't ever have to fear your daughter's sexuality. God created her to develop from a little girl into a grown woman—and he knows what he is doing with his creation! Many dads are terrified of their daughters' physical changes, because they remember the way they used to look at young women when they were teenagers. This explains why some fathers tell their daughters that they can't get married until they're forty. It also explains why they threaten to buy a shotgun (if they don't already have one): they plan to ward off any boys who may come around.

Don't react to your daughter's changes with fear or paranoia. Instead, double the touch. Show healthy affection. After all, your responsibility is to guide your daughter through these years of budding womanhood with love, wisdom, and strength—not scare tactics!

The Significance of a Dad's Example

The goal of every loving, affectionate dad is to raise a daughter who, when the time comes for her to leave the nest and build a nest of her own, expects nothing less from the new man in her life than to be treated with the same love and tenderness she knew growing up. That's why it's so important for dads to set the right example.

It matters how you speak to your daughter. It matters how you speak to her mother. It matters how you speak about other women. (Have you ever made a comment about some "sexy young thing" on a television commercial? Did your daughter hear you?) Your communication speaks volumes, even when you are not addressing with your daughter

> It matters how you speak to your daughter. It matters how you speak to her mother.

directly. Do you want her to become a woman who is treated as a loved, cherished, respected individual, equal in value to men? Or do you want her to be treated as an inferior creature who is little more than a sex object? Your spoken words, intended or not, help form that answer.

So do your actions, especially at home. When I was growing up, my siblings and I had no doubt that our parents enjoyed each other's company and loved one another deeply. Dad and Mom demonstrated their love through their words, often sharing sweet expressions of endearment that made us smile or little teases that made us giggle. They also demonstrated their love through their actions. They were lavish with their physical affection (as they continue to be today). We always saw lots of hugs, pats, and kisses around our house. As a result, our home was filled with love, laughter, and joy. How wonderful it was to grow up in an environment where family members were comfortable showing wholesome affection, warmth, and fondness toward each other!

I now know that Dad was the one who set the precedent for what I wanted in a husband and a home. The way my father loved and adored my mother was the model of affection I sought for myself. When John came along, he had some huge shoes to fill.

The greatest security any father can give his daughter is to love her mother well. By developing and maintaining a deep, positive emotional connection with your wife, you can prepare your daughter to make healthy emotional connections with the men who will one day come into her life—including, most importantly, her husband. The health of your daughter's future romantic relationships is dependent upon her personal relationship with you *and* what she has experienced at home.

My dad set the example for me, and John, in turn, set the

example for our three daughters. As the girls grew up, John not only built strong, affectionate relationships with each one of them; he also demonstrated in a thousand ways his love, admiration, and affection for their mom. As a result, Angela, Danica, and Ashley developed into beautiful, strong, secure young women with huge expectations for the men they would eventually marry. More big shoes to fill! Now all three are mothers raising daughters—and the legacy continues.

The Importance of a Dad's Time

I love the comment my ten-year-old granddaughter, Madison, made about her father, my son-in-law. "My daddy's name is Rod," she said. "We love to go horseback riding. He's a great dad because he found something that I really like to do, and he takes me out so we can do it together. Once he took me to a hockey game, because he knew I really wanted to do that. I know that my daddy cares about the things that I'm interested in. I love him because he's the best."

Rod is carrying on a tradition that John started years ago with our daughters—and continues to this day, even though the girls are grown and married with children of their own. It's the father-daughter date. John stumbled upon this magnificent method for building father-daughter relationships when our eldest daughter, Angela, was eight years old. Now he teaches about it in seminars all over the world. (Hearing John speak on this topic is what prompted my own dad to take me out on a date, as I shared earlier.)

The idea came to John one day when he was out of town, speaking at a businessmen's convention. Feeling very far from home, he began to think about how much he missed his daughters, and how much of their lives he was missing because of his frequent traveling. The girls seemed to be growing up so fast, yet he was seeing less and less of them. *Something needs to change,* he thought to himself. *Somehow I need to find a way to make more time for my family.*

As he waited in the airport for his flight home, he wandered into one of the little stores on the concourse. Looking around, he came across a beautiful greeting card with a picture of sunshine on the front. Since Angela's middle name is Sunshine, he couldn't help but buy the card for her. That's when a purpose began to form in his mind. Inside the card he wrote, "You are invited to go on a very special date with Daddy." He added the details of date and time, then sealed the envelope. When he finally got home, he sneaked into Angela's bedroom and put the card on her pillow.

Nothing could have prepared him for the excitement and anticipation that card created in the heart of his eight-year-old princess. When the special day arrived, John came home from work to find Angela eagerly awaiting her Prince Charming. When he walked in the front door and looked up, he saw Angela standing at the top of the spiral staircase, beaming in all her royal glory. Wearing her favorite "daddy dress," she was a vision of beauty and hopefulness. Her hair was perfectly coifed, a dab of lip gloss shone on her lips, and her smile conveyed pure joy and delight.

John watched as Angela began to descend the stairs slowly, regally, confidently. We had seen our girls practice this walk down the stairway many times before—we called it the "wedding walk." Suddenly John was hit with the full realization of how important this moment was in his little girl's life. He hurried to the bedroom and changed into his very best suit. Then he gathered his date, took her on his arm, and led her to the car, treating her like the princess she was. (If he had known in advance how huge this event would be for Angela, he would have called for a limousine!)

He proceeded to drive to the finest restaurant in town, where

125

he asked the maître d' for the best table in the house. After being escorted to a quaint candlelit table for two, he and Angela looked at the menu and ordered their dinners. That's when John was struck by a terrifying thought: he had no idea how to communicate with his daughter. How could he connect with the world of an eight-year-old—not to mention an eight-year-old *girl*?

But he was determined, and he pressed forward bravely, asking questions that Angela was delighted to answer. They talked about what she did at recess, what she wanted to be when she grew up, what her favorite memories were from last summer's vacation, who she might marry one day. John was amazed to discover that he was totally engrossed in the wonderful world of Angela—a world that was just as important to her as his grown-up world was to him.

They held hands across the table. Often John found himself close to tears. When the date was over, the happy twosome returned home. It was their first date, but far from their last.

John decided to schedule monthly dates with each of his girls. He put the dates on his calendar weeks in advance; he didn't want the busyness of life to crowd them out. As the months and years went by, the dates continued. Our daughters knew, without a doubt, that they were important to their dad. There was a place in Daddy's heart and in his schedule for them. There still is!

These father-daughter dates proved to be significant future-shapers for our daughters. As they grew up, they knew what they were looking for in a husband. Young men would come along and want to go out with them; but if the boys didn't measure up to Dad, they didn't stand a chance! From John, Angela, Danica, and Ashley learned what it was like to be treated with honor, value, and respect. As a result, they were never attracted to men who treated women in dishonoring or disrespectful ways.

> These father-daughter dates proved to be significant future-shapers for our daughters.

The time that John invested in dating our daughters has paid back tremendous dividends—not only in the girls' lives, but in his own. He has reaped so much blessing by what he has sown, not the least of which is a grateful and appreciative wife! I always felt as if he were taking me on a date when he dated the girls. I knew his huge investment in our daughters was an investment in our home and family.

How to Date Your Daughter

Would you like to adopt the Burnses' tradition and begin dating your daughter? Here are a few pointers that John picked up over the years.

1. Go to a neutral place away from home. On a date it is beneficial to leave the environment of home, where everyone tends to wear the "hats" that define their roles and responsibilities within the family unit. Instead, go to a neutral place such as a restaurant or a park, where you and your daughter can just be friends. The goal is to develop a lasting friendship that transcends roles and duties. This takes time; that's why the earlier you begin, the better. But it's never too late to start!

A growing friendship produces intimacy ("in-to-me-see"). Everyone, including your daughter, has his or her own little world, and it is the privilege of friendship—not necessarily parenthood—that opens the door to allow another person to see inside. By dating your daughter, you have the opportunity to develop a closer bond of familiarity, confidence, and understanding. These qualities open the door and form the basis for lifelong friendship.

2. Remember to listen. Since a father-daughter date is for the purpose of understanding and knowing your daughter, listening is crucial. Many dads feel as if they're carrying the weight of the world on their shoulders, and listening to a little girl jabber on about things that don't seem to apply to that world can be frustrating. I have to admit, I enjoyed watching John as he sometimes struggled to listen to the ramblings of his daughters. He is very much a type-A male. He's all about the bottom line; he's into the headlines, not the fine print. Most females, on the other hand, love to talk about the details of life. Does hearing a lot of detailed, relational, girlfriend-stuff bore you? You will have to get over it, if you really want access to your daughter's heart.

3. Leave your own interests behind. As a dad, you must be ready to leave behind for a few moments your personal interests, your business dealings, your sports allegiances, and anything else that seems especially important to you, in order to focus your attention on communicating effectively with your daughter. Take the time to discover what's important to her. Ask questions and listen to her answers to better understand her world. Talk on her level about issues that concern her. Talk often about things that don't really seem to matter. Do whatever it takes to keep the flow of communication open between you. The more you engage your daughter in conversation, even on topics that seem trivial, the more likely she will be to talk to you when issues come up in her life that *are* important—maybe even critical.

Here are a few questions that may help you gauge how well you're doing:

- Do you know the names of any of your daughter's school friends?

- Do you know what her favorite subjects are? Do you know the names of any of her teachers?

- Do you know what her favorite color is? Her favorite book? Her favorite movie?

- Do you know any of her dreams or passions?

- Do you know what she is afraid of?

- Do you communicate with her on a regular basis? When you talk, do you go past the niceties and press into the heart-stuff?

4. Don't be afraid to get real and be vulnerable. Are you feeling a little queasy right now? If so, you're in good company. A lot of grown men would rather go swimming with sharks or leap off a tall building than make themselves vulnerable with their daughters! But don't let fear stop you. Go ahead and be brave. Do it anyway. You will have a lifetime of blessing as the reward for your courage.

There is so much that you will learn, because your daughter has so much to teach you. With her help, you will begin to see life with childlike innocence once again. You will grow in sensitivity and no longer be afraid of your own emotions. You will discover new things, and you will see old things in a new way: from the perspective of the precious little girl you call your own.

If you want the bottom line, here it is: you need your daughter—and she needs you. After all, she won't be little forever. Girls will be women, you know.

chapter

10

Girls Will Be Mothers

I once read an ancient proverb that beautifully reveals the essence of the role of a father in his daughter's life: "He who has daughters is always a shepherd." A dad leads, guards, and cares for the development of his little girl through infancy and puberty; through the often turbulent years of adolescence; and through early adulthood. But his job doesn't end when he becomes the father of the bride, and he walks his princess down the aisle. A dad's influence continues to have an impact in his daughter's life, even when she becomes a mother herself.

The Influence of a Positive Example

Just ask Angela, Danica, and Ashley. Each of our daughters has married a strong man, and not just in the physical sense. They married men who, like their father, would one day be great examples for their future children. John modeled courage to our girls—the heart-strength to do the right thing in a world of compromise. He never buckled under the pressure to please in order to avoid confrontation. Compromise was not an option; he believed that compromising meant settling for something you *didn't* believe, because you were unwilling to fight for what you *did* believe. His values always stayed firmly in place, regardless of the culture's shifting sands. I know his strength made our daughters feel safe as they grew from childhood to adulthood. It also gave them the confidence to eventually marry strong men of their own, so they could raise healthy, loving families and be the moms they knew they wanted to be.

I have such a vivid recollection of Angela when she was about seventeen years old. She had her eyes set upon a strapping, curly-haired, six-foot-three-inch young man in our church. I realized she had begun to consider in earnest the possibility of one day marrying the handsome Rod Doell when she began making comments about every little child she saw who had a head of curly hair. Suddenly she was noticing something that had never caught her attention before. She was dreaming of becoming a mother one day. She did marry Rod eventually; and yes, they are the parents of two gorgeous children with beautiful curly hair!

I know that long before Angela was ready to consider the possibility of marriage and motherhood, a vision had formed in her heart of what she wanted in a husband: someone who would be an amazing father for the children she would have one day. Her own father had set the example.

Here in her own words, Angela shares about her experience as a daughter who became a wife and mother, and about the continuing importance of her relationship with her dad:

Dad called me from his cell phone yesterday at noon. I work from home and was caught up in a project, typing e-mails and fielding phone calls at the same time. He asked if I was ready to go out for a lunch date. Before I could answer, he announced that he was two minutes away and headed toward my house. I had to laugh; that is so my dad! He lives a big life. He pastors, travels globally, makes important decisions every day, and is respected and recognized in his field. He's a busy guy. To me, though, he is simply Dad. I've never questioned whether or not the issues in my life were too silly or unimportant to share with him. Family is his priority, and my life is richer because of it.

Growing up as the firstborn of three girls, I looked to my dad for unwavering support. Since I was a rather introverted child and teen, I relied on his faith in me whenever my own confidence was lacking. I'm sure there were times when he questioned my abilities, but he never showed any doubt in me. In the reflection in his eyes, I saw only the great potential that my life held before me. He saw value in me and honored it, and that support gave me the boost I needed to try new things and persevere through challenges. If Dad thought something was going to be okay, then it was!

My parents put thought and creativity into developing a distinctly unique and fun family dynamic. My sisters and I knew that our family was the greatest, no question. As the Burns Girls, we definitely had our own unique identity, and we knew that we belonged to something special. Dad has never been one to follow the crowd or worry about what others think of him, and his parenting style has always reflected that. When he was the driver on school field trips, we went through the McDonalds drive-through with the radio cranked up. On Valentine Day, he arranged to have bouquets of flowers delivered to me, Danica, and Ashley in our class-rooms. In high school, he sometimes insisted on walking me to my locker and kissing me good-bye right there, in front of the crowd. I often groaned about some of these things; but truthfully, I loved that Dad was determined to be involved in my world.

My dad had the wisdom to know not to back off during the emotional and turbulent teenage years, when I needed his attention most. One of my most tender memories is of an evening I spent with him when I was about fifteen. My best friend had found another crowd to hang out with, and she was infatuated with a new boyfriend. She was suddenly distant, and I was totally devastated. The drama of friends and relationships is everything to a teenage girl!

Dad let me cry on his shoulder; then he dropped his plans for the evening and took me out to dinner. He listened patiently as I sobbed and sputtered through the entire meal.

Now, you need to understand that Dad isn't necessarily the most emotional person. If there's a problem, he wants to find a great solution—fast. Fix it, make it better, and move on! So it was a big deal for him to sit back, allow me to be a mess, and just listen. The fact is, whenever I felt insecure and lost, I knew I could trust that his love for me was unconditional. That knowledge gave me the security I needed to face the world again with composure and confidence.

Today I am thirty years old and the mother of two. I'm incredibly thankful to have had such a strong role model in my dad. My husband, Rod, and I have adopted many of the parenting techniques that I grew up with. Dad loved my sisters and me fiercely, and he never shied away from demonstrating it. He was big enough to admit when he fell short, and he always allowed us the grace we needed to make mistakes. Our journey together has been a great learning experience, and I'm proud of the relationship Dad and I have today. His continued influence is a blessing to me as a woman, a wife, and a mom. My husband and children are blessed as well. My dad has always been my hero—and he still is.

Reading Angela's words again makes me so grateful for John's character and integrity, as well as the character and integrity of my own father. These two dads have led the way and carved a path that has brought great blessing to me, my family, and now my daughters' families. Certainly, neither my father nor John has been perfect. They have both made mistakes on their journeys of fatherhood. But both have loved their families extravagantly and without reservation. Their hearts have revealed the heart of God's love toward their daughters; and in that place of security, we girls have had the confidence to dream enormous dreams about our futures as women, wives, and mothers. What an incredible gift these two dads have invested in their daughters' lives!

The Power of Unconditional Love

When our second daughter, Danica, was a teenager, she went through a hard season in her life. She struggled with a debilitating eating disorder that not only threatened her dreams of becoming a wife and mother, but also her very life. Her courage to press through to victory has always amazed me. She was, and is, a fighter! It was during this struggle that she began to date her future husband, Chris. No doubt she wondered, *Is this a man who will be able to love me unconditionally through the good times and the bad?* Thankfully, she had the example of her father's unconditional love through those years—a model that helped lead her to a husband who would love her unconditionally too. Chris is a remarkable man who showed courage and strength in the face of adversity. Together he and Danica have forged a fantastic life for themselves and their two beautiful daughters. Danica is a wonderful mother, and she and her father remain very close.

I want to let Danica share a little bit about her struggle and how her relationship with her dad helped her get the victory:

Often I've teased that I deserve much of the accolade for Mom and Dad's parenting wisdom, which they now share all over the world. Growing up, my two sisters together couldn't conjure up half the trouble I created in a day! Thankfully, every challenge I threw my parents' way ended up helping all of us gain the wisdom, insight, and life skills that are now helping so many others.

I was a good kid on the inside, and I knew my mom and dad loved me and believed in me. But somewhere along the way, something went awry, and I stopped believing in myself.

CHAPTER 10: GIRLS WILL BE MOTHERS

I had severe issues with low self-esteem, insecurity, guilt, and even depression. As a result, I developed an eating disorder early in high school that took over a decade to work through. I pulled away from everyone in my world—and the one I pulled the furthest from was my dad.

Dad had provided me with a Christian upbringing, a good family, and a loving home atmosphere. There was no abuse or trauma, nothing to make it easy to point a finger. I've often tried to imagine what those years must have felt like for my parents, and especially for my dad. You love and cherish, you provide and nurture; and still, you watch as someone you love slips away. What more could he have done? What would he do differently now?

His instinct was only natural—to step in as the head of the home and fix the problem. Control what I ate, who I dated, what I read. Pray harder and longer. Talk sense into me. It was only when everything that he tried failed that he became more than a good father to me; he became great.

You see, Dad couldn't fix this one. For a season all he could do was hold me and love me and accept me as I was. As a good father, he had plans and dreams for my life, and it was hard for him to watch me throw them away. But as a great father, he set those plans and dreams aside for a while and allowed me time to be a mess in his arms.

As a great father, he also took ownership of his part of my story. Rarely does a child go astray on her own. The issue is almost always a family one, and every family member owns a piece of the puzzle, whether big or small.

Dad is a classic type-A personality. He's a cut-and-dry, mind-over-matter, get-things-done kind of guy. There aren't very many situations that he can't size up and set straight in a flat second. But with me, there was no quick fix. I was an anomaly to him—introspective, ultrasensitive, and hard on myself. Some of Dad's parenting techniques weren't working for me; they were actually contributing to my decline. That's a humbling thing for any parent to accept—especially a good, loving parent. It took a lot of courage for my dad to admit he needed to change.

I've often said that the difference between a good dad and a great dad is this: a good dad gives all he can; a great dad gives it all too—and then is big enough to accept that it's never quite enough.

CHAPTER 10: GIRLS WILL BE MOTHERS

I watched my dad as he surrendered his pride. He surrendered his opinions, his anger, his fear, and his power over me and the situation. I know it was extremely difficult for him, but he allowed me the space to go through what I needed to go through. I was afraid of being truly honest; I was afraid that I might say something that would hurt my parents, embarrass them, or make me seem ungrateful. Dad took the pressure off of me and gave me the freedom to speak my mind and search for the truth, wherever it led. That freedom was exactly what I needed. I felt validated, safe, unconditionally loved, and no longer afraid. I knew that we were in this fight together, and we would get through it, no matter what we might face along the way.

During those years, whenever things got tough, Dad and I dealt honestly and thoroughly with whatever problems were involved. As a result, no hurts, pains, or unresolved issues were left behind to fester or sting. My memories of the past are memories of a loving father who was willing to do whatever it took to help his daughter. What more could a girl ask for? To this day my dad and I share a unique, wonderful, strong friendship. Because of him, I am a healed, whole woman today. I am also a wife and a mother who can minister to her family without having to deal with any leftover baggage from the past.

For Danica, her relationship with her father was the key to her future as a woman, a wife, and a mother. You can read more about her story and about the lessons of fatherhood that John learned during her struggle in John's book, *The Miracle in a Daddy's Hug.*

The Blessing of Belonging

Okay, Angela and Danica have had their turns. Now here are a few words from our youngest daughter, Ashley, about growing up as one of "Johnny's Angels":

I have the best dad in the whole wide world. Over the course of my life, the things that Dad has done that have made me feel the most loved have been the simple things—the things that have helped me know I belong to a family. This wonderful sense of belonging has been a valuable building block in my life. It gives me confidence today, as I raise children of my own.

CHAPTER 10: GIRLS WILL BE MOTHERS

I know my father was a very busy man when I was growing up, but I always felt that I had a lot of his time. Dad went out of his way to create special one-on-one times, including our treasured daddy-daughter dates. As his life and work got busier, it was harder for him to schedule our special dates; but when it mattered most, Dad was always there. I fondly remember the time he took me out and bought me a tennis racquet. I practiced hard to become a better player, because tennis was something that he and I could do together; it was for us, and only us. I never became much of an expert, but I loved those special times on the court with my dad.

As a family Dad made sure we did lots of fun things together, from riding bikes (dressed in proper biking gear from head to foot) to playing a myriad of board games. For a long time he had my sisters and I convinced that *The Flintstones* was his favorite TV show, because he knew that we loved it so much. To this day he is still famous among my childhood friends for our crazy midnight chili-cheese hot dog runs to the local 7-Eleven.

By giving me the gift of his time, my dad played a major role in shaping my vision of what a woman, a wife, and a mother should be. He is one of the main reasons I am who I am today. Now that I'm a mom raising a daughter and a son of my own, I am putting to valuable use the investments of love he made (and continues to make) in my life.

No, my father is not perfect; but he did do a lot of things right, and I am so very aware of his influence in my life to this day. I love him dearly. What can I say? He's the best!

Have you ever noticed that it's often little things in life that matter most? Mother Teresa once said that people are not so much created to do great things as to "do small things with great love."[1] I find it so beautiful that in Ashley's memory bank, the investment of her dad's time is the thing that stands out most. Her sense of belonging—of having a special place within our family unit—established hope and confidence within her that now helps her to be a better wife and mother. The family really is God's magnificent masterpiece!

The Importance of Knowing Your Heavenly Father

Sadly, many women grow up without the blessing of a loving

family. They are fearful of being wives and mothers because of the hurt and pain they've experienced in broken relationships with their own fathers. As I have ministered around the world, I have met a lot of these women. Many of them feel they can never trust a man. They are terrified that men will hurt their daughters in the same ways their fathers hurt them, whether through absence, negligence, or abuse. In large part my ministry is helping these women know they have the promise of hope and forgiveness with God, their awesome heavenly Father—and that broken hearts and dreams can be restored.

Early in our ministry days, John and I met a beautiful but very broken young woman. Crystal's face carried her pain, and her inability to open up and get close to anyone spoke of a wounded heart that had experienced far too much pain and disappointment. Today I am happy to say that Crystal has the biggest, most beautiful heart you could ever hope to encounter. She is living proof that even if your life doesn't start out great, it can finish great by the grace of God!

I want to give her an opportunity to share some of her story in her own words:

For the past ten years I have been working in full-time ministry in two of America's toughest inner cities: Los Angeles and New York. It never ceases to amaze me—the rough streets I walk down; the hurting people I meet; the doors I knock on, never knowing what I will encounter when they open. The fact that I have been given the awesome responsibility and privilege of sharing the Father's love in these difficult places is ironic, given where I have come from in my life. It is wondrous to me that God is able to use me to share his amazing love with hurting kids, teenagers, and moms.

Every day I meet people who think they don't matter in life. They have bought into the lie that I used to believe—their lives are worthless; and if there is a God, he couldn't really love them. How could he, when they don't love themselves? I know where they are coming from. I know what it feels like to carry shame, rejection, and fear around like trophies. I know what it feels like to think, *No one could or ever would love me*; to wonder, *Is there anything in life besides pain and hurt?*

You see, I didn't know a lot of happiness growing up. At first it was just me and my young teenage mom. She was on her own during a time when being a single unwed mother was considered very taboo. She tells me that my father saw me once when I was a baby, but I have never laid eyes on him nor seen a picture of him.

My mother met another man, and when I was four, my brother was born. Soon after his birth, however, his father left too. Then, a few years later, someone else came into the picture. Three days before my eighth birthday, my brother and I had a new stepdad. While he is the one who gave me my sister (she was born a year into the marriage), he was also the one who brought a lot of unhealthy baggage into our home.

My stepfather was a hurtful, abusive man, full of rage and anger. For the next ten years we lived in a vicious circle of abuse, violence, alcoholism, hatred, bitterness—all the painful things that come from excluding God from your life. I lived each day in so much fear. I never knew what it was like to have a loving father; I never saw faithfulness; I never even saw one happily married couple or one healthy, intact family. I determined that the last thing I wanted to do when I grew up was to get married and have children. Why would I want to be a mom and inflict such pain on another generation?

Thank God for his tender mercies and perfect timing!

I will never forget the day some eighteen years ago—it was Mother's Day—when I first walked in the doors of Victory Christian Centre. For some reason, I kept going back. In the beginning, I would arrive late and leave the services early. I was so hardened, so full of hurt and fear. But over time, I began to realize that I had found a place where I could feel safe. As I listened to healthy Bible teaching, my mind began to be renewed. The healing balm of the Holy Spirit started healing my broken heart. Eventually I was able to look in the mirror and see, not an ugly mistake, but a daughter of the King. Finally I knew I had a heavenly Father who loved me and accepted me just the way I was.

Because of God's wonderful mercy, I was able look back at my life and forgive my mother and stepfather. I realized that both of them had experienced a tremendous amount of sorrow and pain. And as Pastor John and Helen often teach, "people cannot give you what they don't have"; "hurt people hurt people"; and "healed people heal people."

These lessons changed my life. Now my once-painful memories of childhood have been turned into helpful blessings for those moms and kids I meet who have been wounded by the ravages of life. Like so many people, they struggle with having a relationship with God as their Father, because they have had poor relationships—or nonexistent relationships—with their own earthly fathers. I can honestly tell them, "I have the best Father, and you can have him too." I know without a doubt that God really is my Father. He loves me and wants the best for me, and no one can ever take him away from me!

I remember the time when I walking through the church hallway, and I saw Pastor John with two of his daughters. He had his right arm around one them and his left arm around the other, and they were all laughing together. I thought, *Wow, what a great father! He loves his daughters so much, and he would do anything for them.* At that moment my heavenly Father spoke to my spirit and said, "How much more do I love you, and how much more will I do for you if you will let me?"

I love him because he first loved me!

Recently I celebrated my eighth wedding anniversary with my wonderful gift from God, Kenny, my friend and husband, who loves me more than I could have ever imagined. We don't have children of our own, so I'm not a mother in that sense. But in another sense, I am. Each week I pour my life into the lives of hundreds of hurting children and families. All the gifts that have been freely given to me, I now freely share with everyone the Father brings along my path. My relationship with my heavenly Father gives me the confidence and courage to be the woman, the wife, and the "mom" he always intended me to be.

What a wonderful testimony! Crystal's life is a living demonstration that even when you grow up without the unconditional love, support, and example of a strong and caring earthly father, you can still have a full and complete life through the revelation of God as your heavenly Father. Today, because of her relationship with God, Crystal is able to be a "mom" to hundreds of children who live in worlds where fathers are rarely present. She is able to introduce these kids to her heavenly Father—and theirs.

The Father's Perfect Plan

In the Father's perfect plan, all daughters would be raised in loving families with loving earthly fathers who tenderly care for them, gently guide them, and faithfully provide for them. When that doesn't happen, God is more than able to fix the broken lives that are left behind. He can create beauty out of ashes. But pain and heartache are not God's desire for his little girls.

That's where *you* come in. As a dad, you are so important in your daughter's life! To her, you are the difference between a healthy, happy childhood and a painful, broken one. You are the key to her future as a woman, a wife, and a mom.

I believe you want to be the best dad you can be; that's why you're reading these words. Who are the best fathers? They are the ones who know the heavenly Father themselves and who try their best to model his unconditional love through all the stages of their daughters' lives. The fruit of their efforts are healthy girls who become healthy young women, who then become healthy wives and mothers.

There is such a beautiful cycle to family life—healthy moms raising healthy children, who become healthy parents themselves, who raise healthy children. This is the answer to every problem in society today! As a father, your role in this cycle is critical. Allow me to encourage you: love your daughter as your heavenly Father loves you. After all, your little girl may be a mom one day.

A Letter to My Dad

Dear Dad,

How could I ever thank you for being the most amazing father in the world? You are the reason I have such a passion in my heart to write a book like this.

Always *and* forever *are two words that are synonymous with how you have loved me. I want to say* perfectly *too, but that wouldn't be right; after all, you are human. But to me you have been a perfect father—one who has always made me feel as if I were the most special girl in the whole wide world, regardless of how I performed, how I behaved, or how I looked.*

My earliest childhood memories are of being celebrated, cherished, and treasured. I have always felt the warmth of your approval and the strength of your support in every phase and season of my life. When I thought my world would break and life wasn't fair, you were there. When I was celebrating life's happiest moments, I wanted you there.

Today, when I hear the popular song by Josh Groban,

"You Raise Me Up," I think of you immediately. Your love, encouragement, and support have truly raised me up. I'm a better woman, a better wife, a better mother, and now a better grandmother because of you. I love the line, "I am strong, when I am on your shoulders." How true that has been in my life! Having the opportunity to stand on your strong, magnificent, and courageous shoulders has been an amazing privilege. The view is great from up there!

No one arrives at her destiny alone. In my case, you have carried me a long way. Your words, your unconditional love, your example, your love for God, your love for Mom, your integrity in business and in relationships, your passion for people, your enthusiasm for God's house, your love for your family and our families—for all these things and so much more, I thank you, Dad. I honor you and bless you. And I thank God for the blessing he poured into my life when he chose you to be my father.

I love you forever. I love you always!

Helen

Notes

Chapter 1

1. John Maxwell, *Developing the Leader within You* (Nashville, TN: Thomas Nelson Publishers, 2001).

Chapter 2

1. *Thayer's Greek Lexicon*, Electronic Database. Copyright 2000, 2003 by Biblesoft, Inc. All rights reserved.
2. Archibald Hart, *The Sexual Man* (Nashville, TN: W Publishing Group, 2004).
3. Albert Mohler, "The Generation That Won't Grow Up." Crosswalk. com, January 24, 2005. Found at http://www.crosswalk.com/news/weblots/mohler/1308760.html?view=print

Chapter 3

1. Willard F. Harley Jr., *His Needs, Her Needs: Building an Affair-Proof Marriage* (Grand Rapids, MI: Revell Books, 2001), 18, 36.

Chapter 4

1. William Pollack, *Real Boys* (New York: Random House, 1998).
2. Steve Biddulph, *Manhood: An Action Plan to Guide Men to a Better Life* (Sydney, Australia: Finch Publishing, 1995), 8.

Notes

Chapter 5
1. Biddulph, *Manhood*, 8.

Chapter 7
1. "Family Structure and Children's Educational Outcomes." Institute for American Values, Center for Marriage and Families, Research Brief # 1, November 2005. Found at http://www.americanvalues.org/briefs/No1_Nov05.pdf. Also, Bruce Bower, "Where's Poppa? Absent dads linked to early sex by daughters." *Science News Online*, Vol. 164, No. 3, July 19, 2003. Found at http://www.sciencenews.org/articles/20030719/fob2.asp.

Chapter 8
1. The full content of Reese Witherspoon's acceptance speech at the 78th Annual Academy Awards on March 5, 2006, can be found on the official Oscar website at http://www.oscar.com/oscarnight/winners/bestactresscategory.html.
2. "Child Abuse in America: National Child Abuse Statistics." Copyright Childhelp 2006. Found at http://www.childhelpusa.org/resources/learning-center/statistics.

Chapter 10
1. Mother Teresa's full quote can be found at http://www.brainyquote.com/quotes/authors/m/mother_teresa.html.